Novels
The Terrible Threes
Reckless Eyeballing
The Terrible Twos
Flight to Canada
The Last Days of Louisiana Red
Mumbo Jumbo
Yellow Back Radio Broke Down
The Free-lance Pall Bearers

Essays
Writin' Is Fightin'
God Made Alaska for the Indians
Shrovetide in Old New Orleans

Poetry
New and Collected Poems (*1988*)
Points of View (*1988*)
A Secretary to the Spirits (*1978*)
Chattanooga (*1974*)
Conjure (*1972*)
Catechism of D Neoamerican Hoodoo Church (*1970*)

Plays
Mother Hubbard, formerly Hell Hath No Fury
The Ace Boons
Savage Wilds

Anthologies
Calafia
19 Necromancers from Now

New and Collected Poems

ISHMAEL REED

New and Collected Poems

ATHENEUM   *New York*   1989

This book includes poems from three previously published collections by Ishmael Reed: *Conjure, Chattanooga,* and *A Secretary to the Spirits.* Many of these poems have appeared in journals and anthologies, and acknowledgment is gratefully made to the editors of *The Berkeley Fiction Review, River Styx, California Living, The Buffalo Evening News, Up Late: American Poetry since 1970, Wind Row, New Letters, Lips, The Berkeley Poetry Review, Black World, Mark in Time, Yardbird Reader, Umbra, Liberator, Essence, Ikon, Scholastic, For Now, In a Time of Revolution, Where's Vietnam?, Poets of Today, The Poetry of the Negro, 1745–1970, The New Black Poetry, Soulscript, The L.A. Free Press, The Black Poets, Dices,* and *The Norton Anthology of Poetry.*

Some of the material in this book, set to music by leading jazz composers, can be heard on two albums released by Pangaea records: Conjure I and Conjure II (available in LP, cassette and compact disc.)

Atheneum
Macmillan Publishing Company
866 Third Avenue, New York, N.Y. 10022

Library of Congress Cataloging-in-Publication Data
Reed, Ishmael, 1938–
  [Poems]
  New and collected poems / Ishmael Reed.
      p.   cm.
    ISBN 0-689-12004-4
    I. Title
  [PS3568.E365N49   1988]
  811'.54—dc20   88-17579   CIP

Macmillan books are available at special discounts for bulk purchases for sales promotions, premiums, fund-raising, or educational use. For details, contact:
  Special Sales Director
  Macmillan Publishing Company
  866 Third Avenue
  New York, N.Y. 10022

10 9 8 7 6 5 4 3 2 1

Printed in the United States of America

To Carla

I Don't Want To Set the World on Fire;
I Just Want To Light a Flame in Your Heart

Contents

CHATTANOOGA

Conjure

The Ghost in Birmingham

The only Holy Ghost in Birmingham is Denmark Vesey's Holy Ghost, brooding, moving in and out of things. No one notices the figure in antique cloak of the last century, haunting the pool games, talking of the weather with a passerby, attending mass meetings, standing guard, coming up behind each wave of protest, reloading a pistol. No one notices the antique figure in shabby clothing, moving in and out of things—rallies of moonshine gatherings—who usurps a pulpit and preaches a fire sermon, plucking the plumage of a furious hawk, a sparrow having passively died, moving in and out of chicken markets, watching sparrow habits become hawk habits, through bar stools and greenless parks, beauty salons, floating games, going somewhere, haranguing the crowds, his sleeves rolled up like a steelworker's, hurling epithets at the pharoah's club-wielding brigade, under orders to hunt down the firstborn of each low lit hearth.

There are no bulls in America in the sense of great symbols, which preside over resuscitation of godheads, that shake the dead land green. Only the "bull" of Birmingham, papier mâché, ten dollars down monthly terms, carbon copy mock heroic American variety of bullhood, who told a crowded room of flashbulbs that there was an outsider moving in and out of things that night, a spectre who flashed through the night like Pentecost.

He's right, there was.

Not the spook of the Judaic mystery, the universal immersed in the particular. Not the outsider from unpopular mysteries, a monstrous dialectic waddling through the corridors of his brain, but the nebulous presence hidden by flashbulbing events in Birmingham, Metempsychosis stroking the air.

Pragma the bitch has a knight errant called Abbadon, in the old texts the advocate of dreadful policies. The whore, her abominations spilling over, her stinking afterbirths sliming their way towards a bay of pigs,

has a bland and well-groomed knight errant who said that "if we hand
down a few more decisions, pile up paper, snap a few more pictures
by Bachrach of famous people before grand rhetorical columns of the
doric order, perhaps they will stop coming out into the streets in
Raleigh, Greensboro, Jackson and Atlanta (sometimes called the
Athens of the south).

Pragma's well-groomed and bland procurer is on long distance
    manufacturing heroes,
Heroes who bray in sirens screaming in from Idlewild, winging in
    from points south,
Their utterances cast into bronze by press-card-carrying harpies,
    those creatures of distorted reality.

O ebony-limbed Osiris, what clown folk singer or acrobat shall I
    place the tin wreath upon?
When will Osiris be scattered over 100 ghettos?

Heroes are ferried in by motorcycle escorts, their faces cast into by
    Pointillism, by Artzybasheff,
Sculptor of Henry Luce's America.

Introducing the King of Birmingham, sometimes called the
    anointed one,
And receives the tin wreath across Americana banquet rooms,
His hands dripping with blood like a fanatical monk as rebellion
    squirms on the stake.

Introducing the Black Caligula, who performs a strip tease of the
    psyche,
Between Tiffany ads and Vat 69, giving up a little pussy for a well-
    groomed and bland knight errant.

O ebony-limbed Osiris, what knight club tap dancing charlatan
    shall I place the tin wreath upon?
All things are flowing said the poet when gods ambushed gods:
    Khan follows Confucius
    Light follows darkness
Tin wreathed heroes are followed by the figure in antique clothes,
    obscured by the flashbulbing events in Birmingham.
Metempsychosis in the air.

The Jackal-Headed Cowboy

We were—clinging to our arboreal—rustled
by a poplin dude so fast that even now
we mistake big mack trucks flying
confederate crossbones for rampaging
steer, leaping into their sandpaper hides
and lassoing their stubble faced drivers as they roar into
corn flaked greasy spoons.

We span the spic and spanned cesspools
nerves rankling like hot headed guerrillas
bayoneting artery routes and crawling through
our bowels with blades in their teeth.

Our mohair suits, our watches, our horn
rimmed glasses and several telephones
petition us to slow down as we forget
whose soupcan we swim.

We stand at Brooklyn Bridge like
mayakovsky before, deafened by the nuts
and bolts and clogged in the comings and
goings of goings of Usura

We are homesick weary travelers in the
jungian sense and miss the brew of the
long night's pipe.

Our dreams point like bushy mavericks to
hawking game and scattering ripple falls.
We will swing from giant cables as if
they were hemp, hacking away at sky
scrapers till they tumble into christmas
crowds.

We will raid chock full O nuts untying
apron strings crouching stealthily in the streets
breaking up conference rooms sweeping away
forms memo pads, ransoming bank presidents
shoving dollar bills through their mahogany
jaws.

We will sit on Empire Sofas listening to
Gabrieli's fortissimo trumpets blare for
stewed and staggering Popes as Tom Tom mallets
beat the base of our brains.
We will leap tall couplets in a single bound
and chant chant Chant until our pudgy swollen
lips go on strike.
Our daughters will shake rattle roll and slop
snapping their fingers until grandfather
clocks' knees buckle and Tudor mansions free
their cobwebs.
Our mothers will sing shout swing and foam
making gothic spires get happy clapping the
night like blown up Zeppelin.

We will sizzle burn crackle and fry like combs
snapping the naps of Henri Christophe's daughters.
and We will scramble breasts bleating like
some tribe run amuck up and down desecrating
cosmotological graveyard factories.
and We will mash stock exchange bugs till
their sticky brown insides spill out like
reams of ticker tape.
and We will drag off yelling pinching bawling
shouting pep pills, detergents, acne powders,
clean rooms untampered maiden heads finger bowls
napkins renaissance glassware time subscriptions
reducing formulas
—please call before visiting—
—very happy to make your acquaintanceship i'm sure—
and boil down one big vat of unanimal stew
topped with kegs and kegs of whipped dynamite
and cheery smithereens.
and then We will rush like crazed antelopes

with our bastard babies number books mojo goofer
dusting razor blades chicken thighs spooky ha'nts
daddygracing fatherdivining jack legged preaching
bojangles sugar raying mamas into one scorching
burning lake and have a jigging hoedown with the
Quadrilling Sun.
and the panting moneygrabbing landlord
leeching redneck judges will scuffle
the embankment and drag the lipstick sky outside.
and their fuzzy patriarchs from Katzenjammer orphic
will offer hogmaws and the thunder bird and their overseers
will offer elixir bottles of pre punch cards
and the protocol hollering thunder will announce
our main man who'll bathe us and swathe us.
and Our man's spur jingles'll cause the clouds to
kick the dust in flight.
And his gutbucketing rompity bump will
cause sweaty limp flags to furl retreat
and the Jackal-headed cowboy will ride reins
whiplashing his brass legs and knobby hips.
And fast draw Anubis with his crank letters from Ra
will Gallop Gallop Gallop

our mummified profiled trail boss
as our swashbuckling storm fucking mob rides shot
gun for the moon and the whole sieged stage coach
of the world will heave and rock as we
bang stomp shuffle stampede cartwheel and cakewalk our
way into Limbo.

The Gangster's Death

how did he die/ O if i told you,
you would slap your hand
                                against your forehead
and say good grief/ if I gripped you
by the lapel and told how they dumped
        thalidomide hand grenades
into his blood stream and/
                                how they injected
a cyst into his spirit the size of an egg
which grew and grew until floating
        gangrene encircled the globe
and/ how guerrillas dropped from trees like
mean pythons
                        and squeezed out his life
so that jungle birds fled their perches/
so that hand clapping monkeys   tumbled
        from branches and/
how twelve year olds snatched B-52's
        from the skies with their bare hands and/
how betty grable couldn't open a hershey bar
        without the wrapper exploding and/
how thin bent women wrapped bicycle chains
        around their knuckles saying
        we will fight until the last bra or/
        give us bread or shoot us/ and/
how killing him became child's play
in Danang in Mekong in Santo Domingo

                and how rigor mortis was sprinkled
in boston soups
                        giving rum running families
stiff back aches

so that they were no longer able to sit
at the elbows of the president
with turkey muskets   or/ sit
on their behinds watching the boat races
off Massachusetts through field glasses but/
how they found their duck pants
          pulled off in the get-back-in-the-alleys
          of the world and/
how they were routed by the people
          spitting into their palms
          just waiting to use those lobster pinchers
          or smash that martini glass and/
how they warned him
                              and gave him a chance
          with no behind the back dillinger
          killing by flat headed dicks but/
how they held megaphones
                              in their fists
          saying   come out with your hands up and/
how refusing to believe the jig was up
          he accused them
                              of apocalyptic barking
          saying out of the corner of his mouth
          come in and get me and/
how they snagged at his khaki legs
          until their mouths were full
          of ankles and calves and/
how they sank their teeth into his swanky jugular
          getting the sweet taste of max factor
          on their tongues and/
how his screams were so loud
          that the skins of eardrums blew off
          and blood trickled
                              down the edges of mouths

and people got hip to his aliases/
                              i mean/
democracy and freedom began bouncing
all over the world
                    like bad checks
as people began scratching their heads

and stroking their chins
as his rhetoric stuck in his fat throat
         while he quoted
men with frills on their wrists
and fake moles on their cheeks
and swans on their snuff boxes
       who sit in Gilbert Stuart's portraits
       talking like baroque clocks/
       who sit talking turkey talk
   to people who say   we don't want
                         to hear it
as they lean over their plows reading Mao
wringing the necks of turkeys
       and making turkey talk gobble
       in upon itself
in Mekong and Danang and Santo Domingo
and

Che Guevara made personal appearances everywhere

Che Guevara in Macy's putting incendiary flowers
on marked down hats   and women
scratching out each other's eyes over ambulances
Che Guevara in Congress putting TNT shavings
in the ink wells   and politicians
tripped over their jowls trying to get away
Che Guevara in small towns and hamlets
where cans jump from the hands of stock clerks
    in flaming super markets/
where skyrocketing devil's food cakes
    contain the teeth of republican bankers/
where the steer of gentleman farmers
    shoot over the moon like beefy missiles
                 while undeveloped people
stand in road shoulders saying
fly Che fly bop   a few for us
       put cement on his feet
       and take him for a ride

O Walt Whitman
visionary of leaking faucets
great grand daddy of drips
    you said I hear america singing
but/ how can you sing when your throat is slit
and O/ how can you see when your head bobs
    in a sewer
in Danang and Mekong and Santo Domingo

and look at them weep for a stiff/
                            i mean
a limp dead hood
Bishops humping their backsides/
folding their hands in front of their noses
forming a human carpet for a zombie
men and women looking like sick dust mops/
    running their busted thumbs
    across whiskey headed guitars/
weeping into the evil smelling carnations
    of Baby Face McNamara
    and Killer Rusk
whose arms are loaded with hijacked rest
in peace wreaths and/
look at them hump this stiff in harlem/
sticking out their lower lips/
and because he two timed them/
        midget manicheans shaking their fists
        in bullet proof telephone booths/
        dialing legbar on long distance
        receiving extra terrestrial sorry
                            wrong number
seeing big nosed black people land in space ships/
seeing swamp gas/
shoving inauthentic fireballs down their throats/
bursting their lungs on existentialist rope skipping/
        look at them mourn/
drop dead egalitarians and CIA polyglots
    crying into their bill folds
    we must love one another or die
while little boys wipe out whole regiments with bamboo sticks
while wrinkled face mandarins store 17 megatons in Haiku

for people have been holding his death birds
on their wrists and his death birds
make their arms sag with their filthy nests
and his death birds at their baby's testicles
and they got sick and fed up
with those goddamn birds
and they brought their wrists together and blew/
                                        i mean/

puffed their jaws and blew and shooed
   these death birds his way
and he is mourned by
drop dead egalitarians and CIA polyglots and
midget manicheans and Brooks Brothers Black People
   throwing valentines at crackers
      for a few spoons by Kirk's old Maryland engraved/
      for a look at Lassie's purple tongue/
      for a lock of roy rogers' hair/
      for a Lawrence Welk champagne bubble

as for me/ like the man said
i'm always glad when the chickens come home to roost

The Feral Pioneers

FOR DANCER

I rise at 2 a.m. these mornings, to
polish my horns; to see if the killing
has stopped. It is still snowing outside;
it comes down in screaming white
clots.

We sleep on the floor. I popped over
the dog last night & we ate it with
roots & berries.

The night before, lights of a
wounded coyote I found in
the pass.
(The horse froze weeks ago)

Our covered wagons be trapped
in strange caverns of the world.
Our journey, an entry in the thirty-
year old Missourian's '49 Diary.
   'All along the desert road from the
   very start, even the wayside was strewed
   with dead bodies of oxen, mules & horses
   & the stench was horrible.'

America, the mirage of a
naked prospector, with sand
in the throat, crawls thru
the stink.
Will never reach the Seven Cities.
Will lie in ruins of
once great steer.

I return to the cabin's
warmest room; Pope Joan is
still asleep. I lie down, my hands
supporting my head.

In the window, an apparition,
Charles Ives:
tears have pressed white hair
to face.

was a-going down, outlaw alias copped my stance
ody greenhorns were making me dance;
my mouth's
g iron got its chambers jammed.

cowboy in the boat of Ra. Boning-up in
West i bide my time. You should see
off these tin cans whippersnappers. I
e motown long plays for the comeback of
Make them up when stars stare at sleeping
t here near the campfire. Women arrive
backs of goats and throw themselves on
vie.

cowboy in the boat of Ra. Lord of the lash,
p Garou Kid. Half breed son of Pisces and
s. I hold the souls of men in my pot. I do
y boogie with scorpions. I make the bulls
ll and was the first swinger to grape the taste.

cowboy in his boat. Pope Joan of the
. C/mere a minute willya doll?
od girl and
e my Buffalo horn of black powder
e my headdress of black feathers
e my bones of Ju-Ju snake
ny eyelids of red paint.
e my shadow

ng into town after Set

cowboy in the boat of Ra

Set   here i come Set
et   to sunset Set
t Set   to Set down Set

    usurper of the Royal couch
    —imposter RAdio of Moses' bush
    party pooper O hater of dance
    vampire outlaw of the milky way

Instructions to a Princess

FOR TIM

it is like the plot of an ol
novel. yr mother comes down
from the attic at midnite & tries
on weird hats. i sit in my study
the secret inside me. i deal it
choice pieces of my heart. down
in the village they gossip abt
the new bride.
i have been saving all this
love for you my dear. if my
house burns down, open my face
& you will be amazed.

There's a Whale in my Thigh

There's a whale in my thigh. at
nite he swims the 7 seas. on
cold days i can feel him sleeping.
i went to the dr to see abt myself.
'do you feel this?' the dr asked,
a harpoon in my flesh. i nodded
yes in a clinic room of frozen
poetry.
'then there's no whale in yr thigh.'

there's a whale in my mind. i
feed him arrogant prophets.

I am a Cowboy

'The devil must be forced to
(potions, charms, fetishes, etc
and these must be burned.' (
1947, endorsed by the coat-o
letter from Francis cardinal S

I am a cowboy in the boa
sidewinders in the saloons
bit my forehead   like
the untrustworthiness of
who do not know their tr
dog-faced man? they aske
from town.

School marms with halito
the Nefertiti fake chipped
germans, the hawk behind
the ritual beard of his axe;
its bells thru the Field of

I am a cowboy in the boat
down with Isis, Lady of th
down deep in her horny, s
in daring midday getaway.
blue,' I said from top of m

I am a cowboy in the boat
of the Chisholm Trail. To
blew off my thumb. Alche
sucker for the right cross.

I am a cowboy in the boat
the temple i bide my time.

poster
and m
    whi
shoot

I am
the o
me pi
write
Osiri
steer
on th
my

I am
the
Aqu
the
keep

I am
Ptah
Be
brin
brin
brin
go
Ha

I'm

I a

loo
to
to

Black Power Poem

A spectre is haunting america—the spectre of neo-hoodooism.
all the powers of old america have entered into a holy alli
ance to exorcise this spectre: allen ginsberg timothy leary
richard nixon edward teller billy graham time magazine the
new york review of books and the underground press.

may the best church win. shake hands now and come
out conjuring

Neo-HooDoo Manifesto

Neo-HooDoo is a "Lost American Church" updated. Neo-HooDoo is the music of James Brown without the lyrics and ads for Black Capitalism. Neo-HooDoo is the 8 basic dances of 19th-century New Orleans' *Place Congo*—the Calinda the Bamboula the Chacta the Babouille the Conjaille the Juba the Congo and the VooDoo—modernized into the Philly Dog, the Hully Gully, the Funky Chicken, the Popcorn, the Boogaloo and the dance of great American choreographer Buddy Bradley.

Neo-HooDoos would rather "shake that thing" than be stiff and erect. (There were more people performing a Neo-HooDoo sacred dance, the Boogaloo, at Woodstock than chanting Hare Krishna . . . Hare Hare!) All so-called "Store Front Churches" and "Rock Festivals" receive their matrix in the HooDoo rites of Marie Laveau conducted at New Orleans' Lake Pontchartrain, and Bayou St. John in the 1880s. The power of HooDoo challenged the stability of civil authority in New Orleans and was driven underground where to this day it flourishes in the Black ghettos throughout the country. Thats why in Ralph Ellison's modern novel *Invisible Man* New Orleans is described as "The Home of Mystery." "Everybody from New Orleans got that thing," Louis Armstrong said once.

HooDoo is the strange and beautiful "fits" the Black slave Tituba gave the children of Salem. (Notice the arm waving ecstatic females seemingly possessed at the "Pentecostal," "Baptist," and "Rock Festivals," [all fronts for Neo-HooDoo]). The reason that HooDoo isn't given the credit it deserves in influencing American Culture is because the students of that culture both "overground" and "underground" are uptight closet Jeho-vah revisionists. They would assert the American and East Indian and Chinese thing before they would the Black thing. Their spiritual leaders Ezra Pound and T. S. Eliot hated Africa and "Darkies." In Theodore Roszak's book—*The Making of a Counter Culture*—there is barely any mention of the Black influence on this culture even though its members dress like Blacks talk like Blacks walk like Blacks, gesture like Blacks wear Afros and indulge in Black music and dance (Neo-HooDoo).

Neo-HooDoo is sexual, sensual and digs the old "heathen" good good loving. An early American HooDoo song says:

> Now lady I ain't no mill man
> Just the mill man's son
> But I can do your grinding
> till the mill man comes

Which doesn't mean that women are treated as "sexual toys" in Neo-HooDoo or as one slick Jeho-vah Revisionist recently said, "victims of a raging hormone imbalance." Neo-HooDoo claims many women philosophers and theoreticians which is more than ugh religions Christianity and its offspring Islam can claim. When our theoretician Zora Neale Hurston asked a *Mambo* (a female priestess in the Haitian VooDoo) a definition of VooDoo the Mambo lifted her skirts and exhibited her Erzulie Seal, her Isis seal. Neo-HooDoo identifies with Julia Jackson who stripped HooDoo of its oppressive Catholic layer—Julia Jackson said when asked the origin of the amulets and talismans in her studio, "I make all my own stuff. It saves money and it's as good. People who has to buy their stuff ain't using their heads."

Neo-HooDoo is not a church for egotripping—it takes its "organization" from Haitian VooDoo of which Milo Rigaud wrote:

Unlike other established religions, there is no hierarchy of bishops, archbishops, cardinals, or a pope in VooDoo. Each oum'phor is a law unto itself, following the traditions of Voo-Doo but modifying and changing the ceremonies and rituals in various ways. Secrets of VooDoo.

Neo-HooDoo believes that every man is an artist and every artist a priest. You can bring your own creative ideas to Neo-HooDoo. Charlie "Yardbird (Thoth)" Parker is an example of the Neo-HooDoo artist as an innovator and improvisor.

Neo-HooDoo, Christ the landlord deity ("render unto Caesar") is on probation. This includes "The Black Christ" and "The Hippie Christ." Neo-HooDoo tells Christ to get lost. (Judas Iscariot holds an honorary degree from Neo-HooDoo.)

Whereas at the center of Christianity lies the graveyard the organ-drone and the cross, the center of Neo-HooDoo is the drum the anhk and the Dance. So Fine, Barefootin, Heard it Through The Grapevine, are all Neo-HooDoos.

Neo-HooDoo has "seen a lot of things in this old world."

Neo-HooDoo borrows from Ancient Egyptians (ritual accessories of Ancient Egypt are still sold in the House of Candles and Talismans on Stanton Street in New York, the Botanical Gardens in East Harlem, and Min and Mom on Haight Street in San Francisco, examples of underground centers found in ghettos throughout America).

Neo-HooDoo borrows from Haiti Africa and South America. Neo-HooDoo comes in all styles and moods.

Louis Jordon Nellie Lutcher John Lee Hooker Ma Rainey Dinah Washington the Temptations Ike and Tina Turner Aretha Franklin Muddy Waters Otis Redding Sly and the Family Stone B.B. King Junior Wells Bessie Smith Jelly Roll Morton Ray Charles Jimi Hendrix Buddy Miles the 5th Dimension the Chambers Brothers Etta James and acolytes Creedance Clearwater Revival the Flaming Embers Procol Harum are all Neo-HooDoos. Neo-HooDoo never turns down pork. In fact Neo-HooDoo is the Bar-B-Cue of Amerika. The Neo-HooDoo cuisine is Geechee Gree Gree Verta Mae's *Vibration Cooking*. (Ortiz Walton's Neo-HooDoo Jass Band performs at the Native Son Restaurant in Berkeley, California. Joe Overstreet's Neo-HooDoo exhibit will happen at the Berkeley Gallery Sept. 1, 1970 in Berkeley.)

Neo-HooDoo ain't Negritude. Neo-HooDoo never been to France. Neo-HooDoo is "your Mama" as Larry Neal said. Neo-HooDoos Little Richard and Chuck Berry nearly succeeded in converting the Beatles. When the Beatles said they were more popular than Christ they seemed astonished at the resulting outcry. This is because although they could feebly through amplification and technological sham "mimic" (as if Little Richard and Chuck Berry were Loa [Spirits] practicing ventriloquism on their "Horses") the Beatles failed to realize that they were conjuring the music and ritual (although imitation) of a Forgotten Faith, a traditional enemy of Christianity which Christianity the Cop Religion has had to drive underground each time they

meet. Neo-HooDoo now demands a rematch, the referees were bribed
and the adversary had resin on his gloves.

The Vatican Forbids Jazz Masses in Italy
Rome, Aug. 6 (UPI)—The Vatican today barred jazz and popular music
from masses in Italian churches and forbade young Roman Catholics to change
prayers or readings used on Sundays and holy days.
It said such changes in worship were "eccentric and arbitrary."
A Vatican document distributed to all Italian bishops did not refer to
similar experimental masses elsewhere in the world, although Pope Paul VI
and other high-ranking churchmen are known to dislike the growing tendency
to deviate from the accepted form of the mass.
Some Italian churches have permitted jazz masses played by combos
while youthful worshipers sang such songs as "We Shall Overcome."
Church leaders two years ago rebuked priests who permitted such ex-
periments. The New York Times, August 7, 1970.

Africa is the home of the loa (Spirits) of Neo-HooDoo although we
are building our own American "pantheon." Thousands of "Spirits"
(Ka) who would laugh at Jeho-vah's fury concerning "false idols"
(translated everybody else's religion) or "fetishes." Moses, Jeho-vah's
messenger and zombie swiped the secrets of VooDoo from old Jethro
but nevertheless ended up with a curse. (Warning, many White "Black
delineators" who practiced HooDoo VooDoo for gain and did not
"feed" the Black Spirits of HooDoo ended up tragically. Bix Beider-
becke and Irene Castle (who exploited Black Dance in the 1920s and
relished in dressing up as a Nun) are examples of this tragic tendency.

Moses had a near heart attack when he saw his sons dancing nude
before the Black Bull God Apis. They were dancing to a "heathen
sound" that Moses had "heard before in Egypt" (probably a mixture
of Sun Ra and Jimmy Reed played in the nightclub district of ancient
Egypt's "The Domain of Osiris"—named after the god who enjoyed
the fancy footwork of the pigmies).

The continuing war between Moses and his "Sons" was recently acted
out in Chicago in the guise of an American "trial."

I have called Jeho-vah (most likely Set the Egyptian Sat-on [a pun on
the fiend's penalty] Satan) somewhere "a party-pooper and hater of

dance." Neo-HooDoos are detectives of the metaphysical about to make a pinch. We have issued warrants for a god arrest. If Jeho-vah reveals his real name he will be released on his own recognizance de-horned and put out to pasture.

A dangerous paranoid pain-in-the-neck a CopGod from the git-go, Jeho-vah was the successful law and order candidate in the mytho-logical relay of the 4th century A.D. Jeho-vah is the God of punish-ment. The H-Bomb is a typical Jeho-vah "miracle." Jeho-vah is why we are in Vietnam. He told Moses to go out and "subdue" the world.

There has never been in history another such culture as the Western civilization—a culture which has practiced the belief that the physical and social environment of man is subject to rational manipulation and that history is subject to the will and action of man; whereas central to the traditional cultures of the rivals of Western civilization, those of Africa and Asia, is a belief that it is environment that dominates man. The Politics of Hysteria, *Edmund Stillman and William Pfaff.*

"Political leaders" are merely altar boys from Jeho-vah. While the targets of some "revolutionaries" are Laundromats and candy stores, Neo-HooDoo targets are TV the museums the symphony halls and churches art music and literature departments in Christianizing (ed-ucation I think they call it!) universities which propagate the Art of Jeho-vah—much Byzantine Middle Ages Renaissance painting of Jeho-vah's "500 years of civilization" as Nixon put it are Jeho-vah prop-aganda. Many White revolutionaries can only get together with 3rd world people on the most mundane "political" level because they are of Jeho-vah's party and don't know it. How much Black music do so-called revolutionary underground radio stations play. On the other hand how much Bach?

Neo-HooDoos are Black Red (Black Hawk an American Indian was an early philosopher of the HooDoo Church) and occasionally White (Madamemoiselle Charlotte is a Haitian Loa [Spirit]).

Neo-HooDoo is a litany seeking its text
Neo-HooDoo is a Dance and Music closing in on its words
Neo-HooDoo is a Church finding its lyrics
Cecil Brown Al Young Calvin Hernton
David Henderson Steve Cannon Quincy Troupe

Ted Joans Victor Cruz N. H. Pritchard Ishmael Reed
Lennox Raphael Sarah Fabio Ron Welburn are Neo-
HooDoo's "Manhattan Project" of writing . . .

A Neo-HooDoo celebration will involve the dance music
and poetry of Neo-HooDoo and whatever ideas the
participating artists might add. A Neo-HooDoo seal
is the Face of an Old American Train.
Neo-HooDoo signs are everywhere!
Neo-HooDoo is the Now Locomotive swinging
up the Tracks of the American Soul.

Almost 100 years ago HooDoo was forced to say
Goodbye to America. Now HooDoo is
back as Neo-HooDoo
You can't keep a good church down!

The Neo-HooDoo Aesthetic

Gombo Févi

   A whole chicken—if chicken cannot be
had, veal will serve instead; a little ham;
crabs, or shrimps, or both, according to the
taste of the consumer; okra according to the
quantity of soup needed; onions, garlic, parsley,
red pepper, etc. Thicken with plenty of rice.
(Don't forget to cut up the gombo or okra.)

Gombo Filé

   Same as above except the okra is
pul-verised and oysters are used

   Why do I call it "The Neo-HooDoo
   Aesthetic"?

   *The proportions of ingredients used depend
upon the cook!*

Sermonette

a poet was busted by a topless judge
his friends went to morristwn nj & put
black powder on his honah's doorstep
black powder into his honah's car
black powder on his honah's briefs
tiny dolls into his honah's mind

by nightfall his honah could a go go no mo
his dog went crazy & ran into a crocodile
his widow fell from a wall &
hanged herself
his daughter was run over by a black man
cming home for the wakes the two boys
skidded into mourning
all the next of kin's teeth fell out

gimmie dat ol time
                religion

it's good enough
        for me!

Mojo Queen of the Feathery Plumes

Why do you want me to slap you
before I make love to you, then
wonder why I do you like I do?

Dark Lady at Koptos, strange lady
at Koptos, Mojo Queen of the
Feathery Plumes

Crawling, pleading and being
kittenish are no habits of the
world's rare cat; shut up in
the mind's dark cage; prowling
in a garden of persimmon, mangoes
and the long black python

Dark Lady at Koptos, strange lady
at Koptos, Mojo Queen of the
Feathery Plumes

When the hunter comes his gleaming
blue coat will galvanize him; his
pearls of sabre teeth will electrify
him; his avocado-green claws will
expose his guts

Dark Lady at Koptos, strange lady
at Koptos, Mojo Queen of the
Feathery Plumes

The scout will run back thru
the forest; 4 Thieves Vinegar
on his tail; the whole safari
not far behind his trail; the dolls
left behind will bare your face;
and the cloth on the bush will be
your lace; you are the jeweler's Ruby
that has fled its case

Dark Lady at Koptos, strange lady
at Koptos, Mojo Queen of the Feathery
Plumes

The cat was dying to meet you
in the flesh but you never came
he wanted you wild but you wanted
him tame, why is your highness afraid
of the night?

Dark Lady at Koptos, strange lady at Koptos
Mojo Queen of the Feathery Plumes

The Black Cock

FOR JIM HENDRIX, HOODOO FROM HIS
NATURAL BORN

He frightens all the witches and the dragons in their lair
He cues the clear blue daylight and He gives the night its dare
He flaps His wings for warning and He struts atop a mare
for when He crows they quiver and when He comes they flee

In His coal black plumage and His bright red crown
and His golden beaked fury and His calculated frown
in His webbed footed glory He sends Jehovah down
for when He crows they quiver and when He comes they flee

O they dance around the fire and they boil the gall of wolves
and they sing their strange crude melodies and play their
weirder tunes and the villagers close their windows and the grave-
yard starts to heave and the cross wont help their victims and
the screaming fills the night and the young girls die with
open eyes and the skies are lavender light
but when He crows they quiver and when He comes they flee

Well the sheriff is getting desperate as they go their nature's way
killing cattle smothering infants slaughtering those who block their
    way
and the countryside swarms with numbness as their magic circle
    grows
but when He crows they tremble and when He comes they flee

Posting hex-signs on their wagons simple worried farmers pray
passing laws and faking justice only feed the witches brew
violet stones are rendered helpless drunken priests are helpless too
but when He crows they quiver and when He comes they flee

We have seen them in their ritual we have catalogued their crimes
we are weary of their torture but we cannot bring them down
their ancient hoodoo enemy who does the work, the trick,
strikes peril in their dead fiend's hearts and pecks their flesh to
    quick
love Him feed Him He will never let you down
for when He crows they quiver and when He comes they frown

Betty's Ball Blues

Betty took the ring
from her fabled Jellyroll
Betty took the ring
from her fabled Jellyroll
She gave it all to Dupree
and eased it on his soul

She climbed his ancient redwood
and sang out from his peak
She climbed his ancient redwood
and sang out from his peak
She thrilled his natural forest
and made his demon creep

She shook the constellations
and dazzled them cross his eyes
She shook the constellations
and dazzled them cross his eyes
She showered his head with quasars
and made his Taurus cry

China China China
Come blow my China horn
China China China
Come blow my China horn
Telegraph my indigo skyship
and make its voyage long

Betty touched his organ
made his cathedral rock
Betty touched his organ
made his cathedral rock
His worshippers moaned
and shouted, His
stained glass windows cracked

One night she dressed
in scarlet and threw
her man a Ball
One night she dressed
in scarlet and threw
her man a Ball
The Butlers came as
zombies, the
guests walked thru
the walls

Dupree he shot the
jeweler, She had him
under a spell,
Dupree he shot the
jeweler, She had him
under a spell

The calmest man in
Sing-Sing is happy
in his cell

The Wardrobe Master of Paradise

He pins the hems of Angels and
He dresses them to kill
He has no time for fashion
No money's in His till
You wont see Him in Paris
or in a New York store
He's the wardrobe master
of Paradise; He keeps right
on His toes

He works from ancient patterns
He doesn't mind they bore
His models have no measurements
His buyers never roar
He never cares to gossip
He works right on the floor
He's the wardrobe master
of Paradise; He keeps right
on His toes

The evil cities burn to
a crisp, from where His
clients go; their eyes
are blood red carnage, their
purpose never fluffed,
His customers total seven
they have no time to pose
He's the wardrobe master
of Paradise; He keeps right
on His toes

He does not sweat the phony
trends, or fashions dumb
decree; His style is always
chic and in, He never takes
a fee
In Vogue or Glamour or Harper's
Bazaar; He's never written up
He's the wardrobe master
of Paradise; He keeps right
on His toes

The ups and downs of Commerce
His shop will not effect:
the whims of a fickle market
the trifles of jet-sets
The society editor would
rather die than ask Him for
a tip; He sews uninterrupted
He isn't one for quips
His light burns in the pit-black night
I've never seen Him doze
He's the wardrobe master
of Paradise; He keeps right
on His toes

Catechism of d Neoamerican Hoodoo Church

a little red wagon for d black bureaucrat
who in d winter of 1967 when i refused to
deform d works of ellison & wright—his betters—
to accommodate a viewpoint this clerk thot irresistible,
did not hire me for d teaching job
which he invitd me to take
in d first place.

this is for u insect w/ no antennae, goofy
papers piling on yr desk—for u & others. where
do u fugitives frm d file cabinet of death get
off in yr attempt to control d artist?
keep yr programming to those computers u love so
much, for he who meddles w/ nigro-mancers
courts his demise!

i
our pens are free
do not move by decree. accept no memos
frm jackbootd demogs who wd exile our minds.
dare tell d artist his role. issue demands on
cultural revolution. 2 words frm china where an
ol woman sends bold painters to pick grasshoppers
at 3 in d a.m. w/ no tea, no cigarettes & no
beer. cause ol women like landscapes or portraits
of their husbands face. done 50 yrs ago. standing
on a hill. a god, a majesty, d first chairman.
o, we who hv no dreams permit us to say yr name
all day. we are junk beneath yr feet,
mosquito noises to yr ears, we crawl on our
bellies & roll over 3 times for u. u are
definitely sho nuff d 1 my man.

ii

is this how artists shd greet u?
isnt yr apartment by d river enough? d
trees in d park? palisades by moonlight is
choice i hear. arent u satisfid? do u
want to be a minister of culture? (minister, a
jive title frm a dead church!) dressd in a
business suit w/ medals on yr chest? hving
painters fetch yr short, writers doing yr taxes,
musicians entertaining yr mistresses, sculptors
polishing yr silverware. do u desire 4 names
instead of 2?

iii

    i do not write solictd
    manuscripts—oswald spengler said
    to joseph goebbels when askd to make a
    lie taste like sweet milk.

because they wrote d way they saw it, said
their prayers wrong, forgot to put on their number in d
a.m., got tore dwn in d streets & cut d fool:
men changd their names to islam & hung up d phone on them.
meatheaded philosophers left rank tongues of ugly mouth on
their tables. only new/ark kept us warm that summer. but
now they will pick up d tab. those dear dead beats who put
our souls to d wall. tried us in absentia before
some grand karate who hd no style. plumes on garveys hat
he was.

iv

word of my mysteries is getting around, do not cm
said d dean / invite cancelld to speak in our chapel
at delaware state. we hv checkd yr background. u make
d crucifixes melt. d governor cant replace them.
stop   stop   outlandish customer.

v

i am becoming spooky & afar you all. I
stir in my humfo, taking notes. a black cat
superstars on my shoulder. a johnny root dwells

in my purse. on d one wall: bobs picture
of marie laveaus tomb in st louis #2. it is
all washd out w/x . . . s, & dead flowers &
fuck wallace signs. on d other wall:
d pastd scarab on grandpops chest, he was
a nigro-mancer frm chattanooga. so i got it
honest. i floor them w/ my gris gris. what
more do i want ask d flatfoots who patrol d beat
of my time. d whole pie? o no u small fry
spirits. d chefs hat, d kitchen, d right
to help make a menu that will end 2 thousand yrs
of bad news.

vi
muhammed? a rewrite man for d wrong daily
news. messenger for cons of d pharaohs court.
perry mason to moses d murderer & thief. pr man
for d prophets of SET. as for poets? chapt
26 my friends—check it out. it is all there in
icewater clear.

ghandi? middleclass lawyer stuck on himself.
freed d brahmins so they cd sip tea & hate cows.
lenins pants didnt fit too good,
people couldnt smoke in front of him, on d
train to petrograd he gv them passes to go
to d head.

d new houngans are to d left of buck rogers,
ok buck up w/yr hands. where did u stash
our galaxies?

vii
bulletin

        to d one who put our
art on a line. now odd shapes will nibble u.
its our turn to put u thru changes. to drop
dour walter winchells on u like, i predict
that tomorrow yr hands will be stiff. to d
one who gaggd a poet. hants will eat yr

cornflakes. golfballs will swell in yr jaws at noon.
horrid masks will gape thru yr window at dusk. it will
be an all day spectacular. look out now,
it is already beginning. to d one who strongarmd
a painter. hear d noise climbing yr steps? u will
be its horse. how does that grab u? how come u
pull d sheets over yr head? & last & least o cactus
for brains. u muggd a playwright, berkeley cal.
spring 68. We hv yr photos. lots of them. what
was that u just spat/up
a lizard or a spider?

viii
spelling out my business i hv gone
indoors. raking d coals over my liver,
listening to my stories w/ yng widow
brown, talking up a trash in bars (if
i feel up to it). doing all those things put down
in that odor of hog doodoo printd as
a poem in black fire. i caught d whiff of yr
stink thou sow w/ mud for thots. d next
round is on me. black halloween on d rocks.
straight no chaser.

down d hatch d spooks will fly/ some
will thrive & some will die/ by these
rattles in our hands/ mighty spirits
will shake d land.

so excuse me while i do d sooner toomer.
jean that is. im gone schooner to a meta
physical country. behind d eyes. im gone be.
a rootarmd ravenheaded longbeard im gone be.
a zigaboo jazzer teaching mountain
lions of passion how to truck.

ix
goodhomefolks gave me ishmael. how
did they know he was d'afflictd one'?
carrying a gag in his breast pocket. giving
a scene a scent of snowd under w/ bedevilment.

i am d mad mad scientist in love w/ d dark.
d villagers dont understand me. here they come
with their torches. there goes a rock
thru d window. i hv time for a few more hobbies:
making d cab drivers dream of wotan
cutting out pictures of paper murderers

like d ol woman w/ d yng face
or is it d yng woman w/ d ol face?
take yr pick. put it to my chest.
watch it bend. its all a big punchline
i share w/ u. to keep u in stitches.
& ull be so wise when their showstopper
comes:
      this is how yr ears shd feel
      this is what u shd eat
      this is who u shd sleep w/
      this is how u shd talk
      this is how u shd write
      this is how u shd paint
      these dances are d best
      these films are d best
      this is how u shd groom yrself
      these are d new gods we made for u
u are a bucket of feces before them.
we know what is best for u. bend down
& kiss some wood.
make love to leather, if u
dont u will be offd

x
& d cannd laughter will fade &
d dirty chickens will fly his coop
for he was just a geek u see.
o houngans of america—post this on yr
temples.

DO YR ART D WAY U WANT
ANYWAY U WANT
ANY WANGOL U WANT
ITS UP TO U/ WHAT WILL WORK
FOR U.

so sez d neoarmerican hoodoo
church of free spirits who
need no
monarch
no gunghoguru
no busybody ray frm d heddahopper planet
of wide black hats & stickpins. he was
just a 666* frm a late late show &
only d clucks threw pennies

*false prophet of the apocalypse

Why I Often Allude to Osiris

ikhnaton looked like
prophet jones, who brick
by brick broke up a
french chateau & set it
down in detroit. he was
'elongated' like prophet
jones & had a hairdresser's
taste.
ikhnaton moved cities for
his mother-in-law &
each finger of his hands
bore rings.

ikhnaton brought re
ligious fascism to egypt.

where once man animals
plants & stars freely
roamed thru each other's
rooms, ikhnaton came up
with the door.

(a lot of people in new york
go for him—museum curators
politicians & tragic mulattoes)

i'll take osiris any
time.
prefiguring JB he
funky chickened into
ethiopia & everybody had
a good time. osiris in
vented the popcorn, the
slow drag & the lindy hop.

he'd rather dance than rule.

My Thing Abt Cats

In berkeley whenever
black cats saw dancer &
me they crossed over to
the other side. alan &
carol's cat jumped over
my feet. someone else's
cat pressed its paw against
my leg, in seattle it's
green eyes all the way.
"they cry all the time when
ever you go out, but when
you return they stop," dancer
said of the 3 cats in the back
yard on st mark's place, there
is a woman downstairs who makes
their sounds when she feeds them.
we don't get along.

Man or Butterfly

it is like lao tse's dream, my
strange affair with cities.
sometimes i can't tell whether
i am a writer writing abt cities
or a city with cities writing
abt me.
a city in peril. everything that
makes me tick is on the bum. all
of my goods and services are wearing
down. nothing resides in me anymore.
i am becoming a ghost town with not
even an occasional riot to perk me
up

        they are setting up a
        commission to find out what
        is wrong with me. i
        am the lead off witness

Hoodoo Poem in Transient

1nce a year marie laveau
       rises frm her workshop
       in st louis #2, boards
       a bus & rides dwn to
       the lake. she threw
       parties there 100 years
       ago.
       some
       lake

Monsters From The Ozarks

The Gollygog
The Bingbuffer
The Moogie
The Fillyloo
The Behemoth
The Snawfus
The Gowrow
The Spiro
The Agnew

Beware: Do Not Read This Poem

tonite, *thriller* was
abt an ol woman, so vain she
surrounded her self w/
    many mirrors

It got so bad that finally she
locked herself indoors & her
whole life became the
    mirrors

one day the villagers broke
into her house, but she was too
swift for them. she disappeared
    into a mirror
each tenant who bought the house
after that, lost a loved one to
    the ol woman in the mirror:
    first a little girl
    then a young woman
    then the young woman/s husband

the hunger of this poem is legendary
it has taken in many victims
back off from this poem
it has drawn in yr feet
back off from this poem
it has drawn in yr legs
back off from this poem
it is a greedy mirror
you are into this poem. from
    the waist down
nobody can hear you can they?

this poem has had you up to here
        belch
this poem aint got no manners
you cant call out frm this poem
relax now & go w/ this poem
move & roll on to this poem

        do not resist this poem
        this poem has yr eyes
        this poem has his head
        this poem has his arms
        this poem has his fingers
        this poem has his fingertips

this poem is the reader & the
        reader this poem

statistic: the us bureau of missing persons reports
        that in 1968 over 100,000 people disappeared
        leaving no solid clues
                nor trace   only
    a space   in the lives of their friends

Dualism

IN RALPH ELLISON'S INVISIBLE MAN

I am outside of
history. i wish
i had some peanuts, it
looks hungry there in
its cage

i am inside of
history. its
hungrier than i
thot

Guilty, the New York Philharmonic
Signs Up a Whale

Today the New York
Philharmonic signed up
a whale.
Ortiz Walton Is black
& better than Casals.
Well Ortiz, I guess you'll
have to swim the Atlantic

If my Enemy is a Clown,
a Natural Born Clown

i tore down my thoughts
roped in my nightmares
remembered a thousand curses
made blasphemous vows to demons
choked on the blood of hosts
    ate my hat
threw fits in the street
got up bitchy each day
told off the mailman
lost many friends
left parties in a huff
dry fucked a dozen juke boxes
made anarchist speeches in brad
the falcon's 55 (but was never
thrown out)
drank 10 martinis a minute
until 1 day the book was finished

my unspeakable terror between the
covers, on you i said to the
enemies of the souls

well lorca, pushkin i tried
but in this place they assassinate
you with pussy or pats on
the back, lemon chiffon between
the cheeks or 2 weeks on a mile
long beach.

i have been the only negro
on the plane 10 times this year
and its only the 2nd month

i am removing my blindfold and
leaving the dock. the judge
giggles constantly and the prosecutor
invited me to dinner

no forwarding address please

i called it pin the tail on the devil
they called it avant garde
they just can't be serious
these big turkeys

The Piping Down of God

god is above grammar
a monk once said. i
want to sit on the window
god told the ticket clerk. you
mean next to the window the
clerk corrected. no, on
the window god insisted. the
clouds have a right to
cheer their boss.

the clerk apologized
& god piped down.

Anon. Poster:

poor sam presents at

ESTHER'S ORBIT ROOM

1753–7th Street Oakland California
Reunion of Soul
with the Sensational Team of
Vernon & Jewel
(back together again)
music by
the Young Lyons

American Airlines Sutra

put yr cup on my tray
the stewardess said 40,000
feet up. (well i've
never done it that way. what
have i got to lose.)

i climb into a cab & the
woman driver is singing
along with Frank Sinatra
"how was your flight coming in?"

(another one. these americans,
only one thing on their
minds).

The Inside Track

a longshot if he cracks up in
doors, but 2 to 1 he
flips out on tv. every
time nixon goes before the
cameras, 80,000 bookies
hold their breaths

For Cardinal Spellman
Who Hated Voo Doo

sick
black grass will
grow on his plot and
the goats will eat
& choke on it

and the keeper of the children's
cries
will terrify his neighbors
& gravediggers
will ask for two weeks
off

when will the next one's
brain explode
or turn from meat to
rock

tomorrow
a week
a month from someday
or the next three turns
of the
moon

Dragon's Blood·

just because you
cant see d stones dont
mean im not building.
you aint no mason. how
d fuck would you know.

Columbia

a dumb
figure
skater per
forming to
strauss'
*also spake
zarathustra.*

she stumbled
during the spin.

i saw this today
on wide wide
world of
sports.

no lie.

Treatment for Dance W/ Trick Ending

one cop enters a store
a 2nd cop pulls a cat frm a tree
a 3rd cop helps an ol woman across
    the street
a 4th cop slaps a prisoner

the cop who pulled the cat frm the
tree leaves the store with a package
& whistling walks dwn the street
the prisoner is put into a box away frm
his fellows
the ol woman files a complaint

one nite in 1965 at 3 in the AM i
stumble down second ave.
8 cadillacs pull up in front
of ratner's. it is a shift of
the 9th precinct. coming on duty
the next morning the cobbler
awakes to find his shoes ruined

Back to Back: 3rd Eye

FOR D.H.

Who are you? Napoleon or something? Fresh from Elba, liberating
the countryside? You wonder why cheering throngs don't turn out
to greet you, in Oakland, in Richmond, in El Cerrito, behind the
county courthouse on the telephone book. New York will follow you
like a Westside meatpacking house that barters your heart for free ice.
They keep to themselves out here.

> Marlon Brando's silver hair sells
> Up-America cakes on the weekends.

STOP!

Western Union for Zora Neale Hurston:
> *Moscow has fallen! Please wire Erzulie for triumphant
> march into the art!*

Off d Pig

background:
  a reckoning has left
some minds hard hit. they blow,
crying for help, out to sea like
dead trees & receding housetops. i
can sympathize. i mean, all of us
have had our dreams broken over some
body's head. those scratched phono
graph records of d soul.
we

   all have been zombed along
d way of a thousand eyes glowing at midnite.
   our pupils have been vacant
   our hands have been icey &
   we have walked with d tell tale
   lurch
all of us have had this crisis of consciousness
which didnt do nobody no good
or a search for identity
which didnt make no never mind neither

at those times we got down on our knees & call
ed up the last resort. seldom do we bother him
for he is doing heavy duty for d universe. only
once has he been disturbed & this was to
  put some color into a woman's blues
he came like a black fire engine spun & sped
by khepera
he is very pressed for time &
do nots play

he apologises for being late
he rolls up his sleeves & rests his bird
he starts to say a few words to d crowd.
he sees d priests are out to lunch so he
just goes on head with what he got to do

out of d night blazing from ceciltaylorpianos
    Thoth sets down his fine black self
d first black scribe
d one who fixes up their art
d one who draws d circle with his pen
d man who beats around d bush
d smeller outer of d fiend

        jehovah-apep jumps up bad on d set
        but squeals as spears bring him down

a curfew is lifted on soul
friendly crowds greet one another in d streets
Osiris struts his stuff & dos d thang to words
        hidden beneath d desert

chorus—just like a legendary train that
        one has heard of but never seen
        broke all records in its prime
        takes you where you want to go right fast

        i hears you woo woo o neo american hoo doo church
        i hears you woo woo o neo american hoo doo church
        i hears you woo woo o neo american hoo doo church
        i hears you woo woo o neo american hoo doo church
        amen-ra   a-men ra   a-man ra

General Science

things in motion
hv a tendency to
stay in motion. the
most intelligent
ghosts are those
who do not know
they are dead:

something just
crossed my
hands

Report of the Reed Commission

I conclude that for
the first time in
history the practical
man is the loon and the
loon the practical man

a man on the radio just
said that air pollution
is caused by jelly fish.

What You Mean I Can't Irony?

A high-yellow lawyer woman
told me I ought to go to
Europe to "broaden your per
spective." This happened at
a black black cocktail party
an oil portrait, Andrew Carnegie,
smiling down

White Hope

FOR SHANE STEVENS

jack johnson licked
one pug so, d man
retired to a farm.
never again opened
his mouth save to
talk abt peachtrees
sow & last year's
almanac;

and whenever somebody
say jack johnson,

he'd get that far away
look.

Untitled I

friday in berkeley. the crippled
ship has just returned frm
behind the moon. fools wave
flags on destroyers in the pacific
i am worried abt this dog
lying in the street. he wants
to get some sun. the old man
across the street trims his
rosebush while just 4 blocks
away there is a war. people
are being arraigned
fingerprinted
hauled away to st rita
made to lie on the floor
the newspapers will lie
abt all this. abt these
12 year olds throwing
stones at the cops, they
wanted to get at some sun
no matter what heavy
traffic was coming down
on them

Untitled II

that house has
a pall of bad
luck hovering over
head
i told you
not to go there
anymore. see
what you get?

Untitled III

everybody in columbia
heights speaks french
ever go to a party there?
bore you to tears.

Untitled IV

the difference between
my heart & your
intellect, my un
disciplined way of
doing
things (i failed
the written driver's
test for example)
& your science, is
the difference between
the earth &
the snow.

the earth wears its
colors well. builds them
loves them & sticks with
them

the snow needs no one.
it lies there all cold
like. it greases behind
wolftracks & wingless
dead birds.
it is a hardship on the poor

thinking is its downfall

Gangster Goes Legit

One day he became six eyes.
The tommy gun on the desk,
as many.
he went into the tommy gun
business

This Poetry Anthology I'm Reading

this poetry anthology
i'm reading reminds me
of washington d.c.
every page some marbled
trash. old adjectives stand
next to flagcovered coffins.
murderers mumbling in
their sleep.

in the rose garden the
madman strolls alone. the
grin on his face just
won't quit

Dress Rehearsal Paranoia #2

In san francisco they are
taking up a collection. if
the earthquake won't come
they'll send for it.

Paul Laurence Dunbar in The Tenderloin

Even at 26, the hush when
you unexpectedly walked
into a theatre. One year
after *The History of Cakewalk.*

Desiring not to cause
a fuss, you sit alone
in the rear, watching a re
hearsal.
The actors are impressed. Wel
don Johnson, so super at des
cription, jots it all down.

I dont blame you for
disliking Whitman, Paul.
He lacked your style, like
your highcollared mandalaed
portrait in hayden's
Kaleidoscope; unobserved,
Death, the uncouth critic
does a first draft on your
    breath.

Badman of the Guest Professor

FOR JOE OVERSTREET, DAVID HENDERSON,
ALBERT AYLER & D MYSTERIOUS
'H' WHO CUT UP D REMBRANDTS

i
u worry me whoever u are
i know u didnt want me to
come here but here i am just
d same; hi-jacking yr stagecoach,
hauling in yr pocket watches & mak
ing u hoof it all d way to
town. black bard, a robber w/ an
art: i left some curses in d cash
box so ull know its me

listen man, i cant help it if
yr thing is over, kaput,
    finis
no matter how u slice it dick
u are done. a dead duck all out
of quacks. d nagging hiccup dat
goes on & on w/out a simple glass
    of water for relief

ii
uve been teaching shakespeare for
20 years only to find d joke
    on u
d eavesdropping rascal who got it
in d shins because he didnt know
enough to keep his feet behind d cur
tains: a sad-sacked head served on a

platter in titus andronicus or falstaff
      too fat to make a go of it
      anymore

iii
its not my fault dat yr tradition
was knocked off wop style & left in
d alley w/ pricks in its mouth. i
read abt it in d papers but it was no
      skin off my nose
wasnt me who opened d gates & allowed
d rustlers to slip thru unnoticed. u
ought to do something abt yr security or
      mend yr fences partner
dont look at me if all dese niggers
are ripping it up like deadwood dick;
doing art d way its never been done. mak
ing wurlitzer sorry he made d piano dat
will drive mozart to d tennis
      courts
making smith-corona feel like d red
faced university dat has just delivered china
      some 50 e-leben h bomb experts

i didnt deliver d blow dat drove d
abstract expressionists to my ladies
linoleum where dey sleep beneath tons of
wax & dogshit & d muddy feet of children or
because some badassed blackpainter done sent
french impressionism to d walls of highrise
      lobbies where dey belong is not my fault
martha graham will never do d jerk
shes a sweet ol soul but her hips
cant roll; as stiff as d greek
statues she loves so much

iv
dese are d reasons u did me nasty
j alfred prufrock, d trick u pull
d in d bookstore today; stand in d
corner no peaches for a week, u lemon

Introducing a New Loa

conclude this Work, a great hydrogen cloud, twenty seven million
es long leisurely passes thru this solar system at 40,000 miles per
"The biggest thing yet seen in space." No one knows where it
e from. Another galaxy? This solar system?

it took the small halo of another planet, out to make a rep for
lf, to squeal on it. I claim it as my floating orphan. When i walked
t the FM antenna just now, it called out my name. I respond to
call it the invisible train for which this Work has been but a modest
edule. A time-table subject to change. Greetings from the swinging
oDoo cloud; way up there, the softest touch in Everything; doing
ance they call

"The Our Turn"

u must blame me because yr wife is
ugly. 86-d by a thousand discriminating
saunas. dats why u did dat sneaky thing
i wont tell d townsfolk because u hv
to live here and im just passing thru

v
u got one thing right tho. i did say
dat everytime i read william faulkner i
go to sleep.

fitzgerald wdnt hv known a gangster if one
had snatched zelda & made her a moll tho
she wd hv been grateful i bet

bonnie of clyde wrote d saga of suicide
sal just as d feds were closing in. it is
worth more than d collected works of ts
elliot a trembling anglican whose address
is now d hell dat thrilld him so
last word from down there he was open
ing a publishing co dat will bore d
devil back to paradise

vi
& by d way did u hear abt grammar?
cut to ribbons in a photo finish by
stevie wonder, a blindboy who dances
on a heel. he just came out of d slang
& broke it down before millions.
    it was bloody murder

vii
to make a long poem shorter—3 things
    moleheaded lame w/4 or 5 eyes

1) yr world is riding off into d sunset
2) d chips are down & nobody will chance yr i.o.u.s.
3) d last wish was a fluke so now u hv to re
turn to being a fish
p.s. d enchantment has worn off

dats why u didnt like my reading list—right?
it didnt include anyone on it dat u cd in
vite to a cocktail party & shoot a lot of
      bull—right?
so u want to take it out on my hide—right?
well i got news for u professor nothing—i
am my own brand while u must be d fantasy of
      a japanese cartoonist

a strangekind of dinosaurmouse
i can see it all now. d leaves
are running low. its d eve of
extinction & dere are no holes to
accept yr behind. u wander abt yr
long neck probing a tree. u think
its a tree but its really a trap. a
cry of victory goes up in d kitchen of
d world. a pest is dead. a prehis
toric pest at dat. a really funnytime
prehistoric pest whom we will lug into
a museum to show everyone how really funny
u are
      yr fate wd make a good
scenario but d plot is between u &
charles darwin.

as i said, im passing thru, just sing
ing my song. get along little doggie &
jazz like dat. word has it dat a big gold
shipment is coming to californy. i hv to
ride all night if im to meet my pardners
dey want me to help score d ambush

From the Files of Agent 22

a black banana
can make you high
bad apples can get
you wasted
the wrong kind of
grapes tore up
for days
and a rancid orange
plastered

know your spirits
before entering
strange orchards

Chattanooga

Chattanooga

1

Some say that Chattanooga is the
Old name for Lookout Mountain
To others it is an uncouth name
Used only by the uncivilised
Our a-historical period sees it
As merely a town in Tennessee
To old timers of the Volunteer State
Chattanooga is "The Pittsburgh of
The South"
According to the Cherokee
Chattanooga is a rock that
Comes to a point

They're all right
Chattanooga is something you
Can have anyway you want it
The summit of what you are
I've paid my fare on that
Mountain Incline #2, Chattanooga
I want my ride up
I want Chattanooga

2

Like Nickajack a plucky Blood
I've escaped my battle near
Clover Bottom, braved the
Jolly Roger raising pirates
Had my near miss at Moccasin Bend
To reach your summit so
Give into me Chattanooga
I've dodged the Grey Confederate sharpshooters

Escaped my brother's tomahawks with only
Some minor burns
Traversed a Chickamauga of my own
Making, so
You belong to me Chattanooga

3
I take your East Ninth Street to my
Heart, pay court on your Market
Street of rubboard players and organ
Grinders of Haitian colors rioting
And old Zip Coon Dancers
I want to hear Bessie Smith belt out
I'm wild about that thing in
Your Ivory Theatre
Chattanooga
Coca-Cola's homebase
City on my mind

4
My 6th grade teacher asked me to
Name the highest mountain in the world
I didn't even hesitate, "Lookout Mountain"
I shouted. They laughed
Eastern nitpickers, putting on the
Ritz laughed at my Chattanooga ways
Which means you're always up to it

To get to Chattanooga you must
Have your Tennessee
"She has as many lives as a
cat. As to killing her, even
the floods have failed
you may knock the breath out of
her that's all. She will re-
fill her lungs and draw
a longer breath than ever"
From a Knoxville editorial—
1870s

5

Chattanooga is a woman to me too
I want to run my hands through her
Hair of New Jersey tea and redroot
Aint no harm in that
Be caressed and showered in
Her Ruby Falls
That's only natural
Heal myself in her
Minnehaha Springs
58 degrees F. all year
Around. Climb all over her
Ridges and hills
I wear a sign on my chest
"Chattanooga or bust"

6

"HOLD CHATTANOOGA AT ALL HAZARDS"—Grant
    to Thomas

When I tasted your big juicy
Black berries ignoring the rattle-
Snakes they said came to Cameron
Hill after the rain, I knew I
Had to have you Chattanooga
When I swam in Lincoln Park
Listening to Fats Domino sing
I found my thrill on Blueberry
Hill on the loudspeaker
I knew you were mine Chattanooga
Chattanooga whose Howard Negro
School taught my mother Latin
Tennyson and Dunbar
Whose Miller Bros. Department
Store cheated my Uncle out of
What was coming to him
A pension, he only had 6
Months to go
Chattanoooooooooooooooooooooga
Chattanoooooooooooooooooooooga
"WE WILL HOLD THE TOWN TILL WE STARVE"—
    Thomas to Grant

7

To get to Chattanooga you must
Go through your Tennessee
I've taken all the scotsboros
One state can dish out
Made Dr. Shockley's "Monkey Trials"
The laughing stock of the Nation
Capt. Marvel Dr. Sylvanias shazam
Scientists running from light-
ning, so
Open your borders. Tennessee
Hide your TVA
DeSota determined, this
Serpent handler is coming
Through

Are you ready Lookout Mountain?

"Give all of my Generals what he's
drinking," Lincoln said, when the
Potomac crowd called Grant a lush

8

I'm going to strut all over your
Point like Old Sam Grant did
My belly full of good Tennessee
Whiskey, puffing on
A.05 cigar
The campaign for Chattanooga
Behind me
Breathing a spell
Ponying up for
Appomattox!

Railroad Bill, A Conjure Man

A HOODOO SUITE

Railroad Bill, a conjure man
Could change hisself to a tree
He could change hisself to a
Lake, a ram, he could be
What he wanted to be

When a man-hunt came he became
An old slave shouting boss
He went thataway. A toothless
Old slave standing next to a
Hog that laughed as they
Galloped away.
Would laugh as they galloped
Away

Railroad Bill was a conjure man
He could change hisself to a bird
He could change hisself to a brook
A hill he could be what he wanted
To be

One time old Bill changed hisself
To a dog and led a pack on his
Trail. He led the hounds around
And around. And laughed a-wagging
His tail. And laughed
A-wagging his tail

Morris Slater was from Escambia
County, he went to town a-toting
A rifle. When he left that

Day he was bounty.
Morris Slater was Railroad Bill
Morris Slater was Railroad Bill

Railroad Bill was an electrical
Man he could change hisself into
Watts. He could up his voltage
Whenever he pleased
He could, you bet he could
He could, you bet he could

Now look here boy hand over that
Gun, hand over it now not later
I needs my gun said Morris Slater
The man who was Railroad Bill
I'll shoot you dead you SOB
let me be whatever I please
The policeman persisted he just
Wouldn't listen and was buried the
Following eve. Was buried the
Following eve. Many dignitaries
Lots of speech-making.

Railroad Bill was a hunting man
Never had no trouble fetching game
He hid in the forest for those
Few years and lived like a natural
King. Whenever old Bill would
Need a new coat he'd sound out his
Friend the Panther. When Bill got
Tired of living off plants the
Farmers would give him some hens.
In swine-killing time the leavings of
Slaughter. They'd give Bill the
Leavings of slaughter. When he
needed love their fine Corinas
They'd lend old Bill their daughters

Railroad Bill was a conjure man he
Could change hisself to a song. He
Could change hisself to some blues

Some reds he could be what he wanted
To be

E. S. McMillan said he'd get old
Bill or turn in his silver star
Bill told the Sheriff you best
Leave me be said the outlaw from
Tombigbee. Leave me be warned
Bill in 1893

Down in Yellowhammer land
By the humming Chattahoochee
Where the cajun banjo pickers
Strum. In Keego, Volina, and
Astoreth they sing the song of
How come

Bill killed McMillan but wasn't
Willin rather reason than shoot
A villain. Rather reason than
Shoot McMillan

"Railroad Bill was the worst old coon
Killed McMillan by the light of the
Moon
Was lookin for Railroad Bill
Was lookin for Railroad Bill"

Railroad Bill was a gris-gris man
He could change hisself to a mask
A Ziba, a Zulu
A Zambia mask. A Zaramo
Doll as well
One with a necklace on it
A Zaramo doll made of wood

I'm bad, I'm bad said Leonard
McGowin. He'll be in hell and dead he
        Said in 1896
Shot old Bill at Tidmore's store
This was near Atmore that Bill was
        Killed in 1896.

He was buying candy for some children
Procuring sweets for the farmers' kids

Leonard McGowin and R. C. John as
Cowardly as they come. Sneaked up
On Bill while he wasn't lookin.
Ambushed old Railroad Bill
Ambushed the conjure man. Shot him
In the back. Blew his head off.

Well, lawmen came from miles around
All smiles the lawmen came.
They'd finally got rid of
Railroad Bill who could be what
He wanted to be

Wasn't so the old folks claimed
From their shacks in the Wawbeek
Wood. That aint our Bill in that
old coffin, that aint our man
You killed. Our Bill is in the
Dogwood flower and in the grain
We eat
See that livestock grazing there
That Bull is Railroad Bill
The mean one over there near the
Fence, that one is Railroad Bill

Now Hollywood they's doing old
Bill they hired a teacher from
Yale. To treat and script and
Strip old Bill, this classics
Professor from Yale.
He'll take old Bill the conjure
Man and give him a-na-ly-sis. He'll
Put old Bill on a leather couch
And find out why he did it.
Why he stole the caboose and
Avoided nooses why Bill raised so
Much sand.

He'll say Bill had a complex
He'll say it was all due to Bill's
Mother. He'll be playing the
Dozens on Bill, this
Professor from Yale

They'll make old Bill a neurotic
Case these tycoons of the silver
Screen. They'll take their cue
From the teacher from Yale they
Gave the pile of green
A bicycle-riding dude from Yale
Who set Bill for the screen
Who set Bill for the screen

They'll shoot Bill zoom Bill and
Pan old Bill until he looks plain
Sick. Just like they did old Nat
The fox and tried to do Malik
Just like they did Jack Johnson
Just like they did Jack Johnson

But it wont work what these hacks
Will do, these manicured hacks from
Malibu cause the people will see
That aint our Bill but a haint of
The silver screen. A disembodied
Wish of a Yalie's dream

Our Bill is where the camellia
Grows and by the waterfalls. He's
Sleeping in a hundred trees and in
A hundred skies. That cumulus
That just went by that's Bill's
Old smiling face. He's having a joke
On Hollywood
He's on the varmint's case.

Railroad Bill was a wizard. And
His final trick was tame. Wasn't
Nothing to become some celluloid
And do in all the frames.

And how did he manage technology
And how did Bill get so modern?
He changed hisself to a production
Assistant and went to work with
The scissors.
While nobody looked he scissored
Old Bill he used the scissors.

Railroad Bill was a conjure man
He could change hisself to the end.
He could outwit the chase and throw
Off the scent he didn't care what
They sent. He didn't give a damn what
They sent.
Railroad Bill was a conjure man
Railroad Bill was a star he could change
Hisself to the sun, the moon
Railroad Bill was free
Railroad Bill was free

The Kardek Method

No son, I dont wanta draw
I hung up my *Petro* in the Spring
of '68. Had got done with pick
ing notches; and what with the wing
ing and all, I ask you, was it
worth it?
So uncock your rod friend. Have
a sitdown.
While I stand back about 15 feet
think about some positive things. The
gals at the Road to Ruin Cabaret at the
end of the trail. The ranch in
Arizona you have your heart set
on.
Dont fret the blue rays emanating from
my fingers. They aint gonna cut you.
A-ha. Just as I thought. Your outside
aura looks a little grey. Your particles
cry the dull murmur of dying. I detect
a little green and red inside your
protecting sheet. You are here but
your ghost running cross a desert in a
greyhound. It bought a ticket to
No Place In Particular.
Swoooooooooooooooooooosh!!
Yonder went the Combined Hand Pass
    Feel Better?

Haitians

1

Fell the leader and
Confuse the pack
Nature's way, this
Shaggy, limping buffalo
Is downed by
Fanged schemers with plenty
Of time, a dry, crawling,
Beach fooled a Chief Whale into
Thinking it was a sea

2

We too are taken in like
Fishbelly, Mississippi in
Paris, no sooner had he
Arrived but here they come
The jackals
Camping about his favorite
Cafés
Mooching off of him, the Blackamoors
Bearing tales about him on
A greenback pillow to the
Crew-cutted sheik
Remember?
The Island of Hallucinations

3

The prospect of Bird going
Tenor made saxophones leap
Like it was a Wall Street crash
Many hornmen were wiped out

4
You know, I used to be a
Hyena, many grins ago
Before my cabin door, this
Morning, the naked rooster
In the Georgia Sea Islands our
Brothers and Sisters have a
Cure for this mess. They
Let the sun infuse the print
    Me too

Skirt Dance

---

i am to my honey what marijuana is
to tiajuana. the acapulco gold of her
secret harvest. up her lush coasts i
glide at midnite bringing a full boat.
(that's all the spanish i know.)

Kali's Galaxy

My 200 inch eyes are trained
on you, my love spectroscope
Breaking down your wavelengths
With my oscillating ear
I have painted your
Portrait: ermine curled about
Yonder's glistening neck

They say you are light-years
Away, but they understand so
Little

You are so near to me
We collide
Our stars erupt into supernovae
An ecstatic cataclysm that
Amazes astronomers

I enter your Milky Way
Seeking out your suns
Absorbing your heat
Circumventing your orbs
Radiating your nights

Once inside your heavens
I hop from world to world
Until I can go no longer
And Z out in your dust
Your new constellation
Known for my shining process
And fish-tailed chariot

Poison Light

FOR J. OVERSTREET

Last night
I played Kirk Douglas to
Your Burt Lancaster. Reflecting
20 years of tough guys I
Saw at the Plaza Theatre in
Buffalo, New York. I can
Roll an L like Bogart
You swagger like Wayne

Ours was a bad performance
The audience, our friends
Panned it. The box office
Hocked the producers

We must stop behaving like
The poison light we grew on

Ancient loas are stranded
They want artfare home
Our friends watch us. They
Want to hear what we say

Let's face it
My eye has come a long way
So has your tongue
They belong on a pyramid wall
Not in a slum
("Dead End"; 1937)

The Decade that Screamed

the sun came up
the people yawned and stretched
in rat traps whipping mildewed cats,
pomaded and braced in gold bathrooms of
baroque toilet boxes,
from chairs with paws,
from snuff cases,
from the puzzlement of round square rooms
they poured into the streets,
yelling down phantom taxi cabs,
jostling old men
blowing their noses with tired flags

some came in steel rickshaws
some in buicks
some on weird pack animals
talking extinct words
(linguists bought them kool aid)
some popped gum
some were carried
some grumbled
some fondled pistols
others in trench coats jotted down names
for the state   took photos

babies set up tents
and auctioned off errant mothers
jive oatmeal was flung at finger-wagging humanists
who drew up their hind legs and split for the cafés
covering their faces with *Les Temps Moderne*
with grapefruit and cherries

a famous editor was hanged on the spot for quoting
jefferson with almost no deliberation his credit cards
stamps line gauge correspondence and grey pages
slid towards the sewer

some sprinted
some bopped
some leaned on shaky lamp posts
others sat down
crossed their legs
and marveled
as the old men
talked of what was
talked of what is
talked of what is to come
talked crazy talk
toyed with their whiskers
threw difficult finger exercises at each other
(white lightning)

jumped like birds
jumped like lions
(yellow thunder)

a girl above   on a ledge toes over the edge
knees knocking teeth chattering

      JUMP JUMP JUMP (millions of hands megaphoning
        razored lips)

some danced
some sang
some vomited
stained themselves
pared fingernails

the moon came sick with old testament hang ups
people fought over exits
rain rain on the splintered girl
rain rain on deserted rickshaws, buicks

in certain rooms we ball our fists
"today in Cyprus, gunbattling"
in certain rooms we say   how awful
"today in Detroit, sniper fire"
rain rain on the splintered girl
rain rain on the baby auctioneers

The Katskills Kiss Romance Goodbye

1

After twenty years of nods
He enters the new regime
The machine guns have been
Removed from the block
The women don't wear anything
You can see everything

2

Hendrick Hudson's Tavern
Has slipped beneath the
Freeway where holiday drivers
Rush as if they've seen the
Hessian Trooper seeking his
Head

3

They get their goosebumps at
The drive-in nowadays, where
The Lady in White at Raven
Rock is Bette Davis and
Burton apes Major André
Hanging before the Haunted
Bridge

4

A New England historian has
Proof that King George wasn't
So bad.
Gave in to every demand
Donated tea to the American needy
Yankees are just naturally jumpy

5

Where once stood madmen
Buttonholing you
Gentlemen think of Martinis
On the train to Mount Vernon

6

R.I.P. old Rip
Cuddle up in your Romance
Your dog Wolf is dead
Your crazy galligaskins out
Of style
Your cabbages have been canned
Your firelock isn't registered
Your nagging wife became a
Scientist, you were keeping
Her down

7

Go back to the Boarded Up
Alley and catch some more winks
Dreaming is still on the house

Untitled

law isn't all
The drivers test
Says nothing about
dogs, but people
stop anyway

Antigone, This Is It

FOR FRED

Whatever your name, whatever
Your beef, I read you like I
Read a book
You would gut a nursery
To make the papers, like
Medea your Poster Queen
You murder children
With no father's consent

You map your treachery shrewdly,
A computer
Click clicking
As it tracks a ship
Headed for the Unknown
Making complex maneuvers
Before splashing down into
Mystery

Suppose everyone wanted it their
Way, traffic would be bottled up
The Horsemen couldn't come
There would be no beauty, no radio
No one could hear your monologues
Without drums or chorus
In which you are right
And others, shadows, snatching things

Fate, The Gods, A Jinx, The Ruling Class
Taboo, everything but you
All the while you so helpless
So charming, so innocent

Crossed your legs and the lawyer
Muttered, dropped your hankie
And the judges stuttered

You forgot one thing though, thief
Leaving a silver earring at the
Scene of a house you've pilfered
You will trip up somewhere
And the case will be closed

Standup Antigone,
The jury finds you guilty
Antigone, may the Eater
Of The Dead savor your heart
You wrong girl, you wrong
Antigone, you dead, wrong
Antigone, this is it

Your hair will turn white overnight

And the Devil Sent a Ford Pinto
Which She Also Routed

Sarah was banged &
Slammed & thrown &
Jostled, shook &
Shifted & ripped
& rumpled

D nex day she was on
D freeway

Tennesseeee women

thoroughbreds

Cuckoo

A cuckoo is a funny bird
Ridiculously masked he will
Tickle your tummy with
His quill
He will look like you
And be your brother

He will cheep your old favorites
At the drop of your dime

A cuckoo is a silly thing
Until he eliminates your offspring
And splits your ears with
His origin

Rock Me, Baby

Turning Screw: In wave-guide
Technique an ad
Justing element in the form of
A rod whose depth of pene
Tration through the wall into
A wave-guide or cavity is ad-
Justable by rotating a screw

Mystery 1st Lady

franklin pierce's wife never
came downstairs.   she never
came upstairs either.

To a Daughter of Isaiah

I saw your drumming lover
On the tube last night
His wrists had been riveted
He made faces, like Jazz
Was a dentist
His gutbucket was
Straight from the Academy
That is, you couldn't
Grind to it
(Matthew Arnold, blowing
His nose)

He drummed, I summed
You up while helping white
Wine get better:
Your juicy Ethiopian art
Lips (my, my)
Your moans. What moans!
Even the ceiling over the bed
Got hard

This happened way back in a book
You were my daughter of Isaiah
I was your flail and crook

My Brothers

They come up here
Shit on my floor
Spill my liquor
Talk loud
Giggle about my books
Remove things from their
Natural places

They come up here
And crackle the snot-
Nosed sniggle about
My walk my ways my words

Signify about what is
Dear to me

My brothers
They come up here and
Hint at underhanded things
Look at me as if to
Invite me outside

My brothers
They come up here
And put me on the hot
Seat so I feel I am
Walking the last mile

My wrong, sorry, no
Manners brothers

I will invite them again
I must like it?

You tell me

Contest ends at midnight

The Vachel Lindsay Fault

All wines are
Not the same
Red, nor are
All Bloods

Nothing to
Brood about
But, nevertheless
A dud

Back to Africa

A Tartar Wolf
Spider
Spinning
From the ceiling

Instead of
Squashing
You look
It up

Swift, Tiny and Fine

He can climb vulgar
Like scooting up the
Side of a diamond
Discourse with a phoenix
Sail out to sea in a
Golden-brown doughnut
He can run a rodeo
With ants

   This man
Can make the M in Mc
Donald's a rainbow
Transpose a sonata from
Fiddle to trumpet
Run out to the back yard
Pick a plum, eat that
Plum, run back
Sit down, cross his
Legs, smile
Then hear that sonata
Before it's tooted

Good

What the heck
I'm sick of Roller Derby champeens

A hummingbird standing still in mid air,
Robert Hayden is The Great Aware

Crocodiles

A crocodile dont hunt
Him's victims
They hunts him
All he do is
Open he jaws

Al Capone in Alaska

or
hoodoo ecology vs the judeo-
christian tendency to *let em*
have it!

The Eskimo hunts
the whale & each year
the whale flowers for the
Eskimo.
This must be love baby!
One receiving with respect
from a Giver who has
plenty.
There is no hatred here.
There is One Big Happy
Family here.

American & Canadian Christians
submachine gun the whales.
They gallantly sail out &
shoot them as if the Pacific
were a Chicago garage on
St. Valentine's day

Visit to a Small College

you name your buildings after
john greenleaf whittier. you
left a great critic Nick Aaron
Ford waiting at the airport
for 3 hours. the room i
sleep in is scorching but
when i request an air
conditioner you think it
a joke.

"open the window," you chuckle.

you invited me here but
don't have my books on your
list, or in your
bookstore.

i landed in your town
at 12 midnite & sarah
pointed to the blood on the
moon.

that will teach me to
mark my omens. believing
in future ones and up
dating old ones.
let's see
the president dropped the first
baseball of the season last yr.
what does that portend?

THE LAST STANZA OF WHICH IS A RUSSELLIAN STANZA NAMED FOR ITS BEST CRAFTSMAN— NIPSEY RUSSELL

Many whiskey ads. More even than *The
New Yorker*. Not even the subtlety of
Coolidge, wearing Indian feathers but
Seagram's V.O. covers an entire page.
Does enamel prose drive its readers
to drink? Living in New York? Or
Commentary's exchange of letters be
tween Podhoretz and Kazin? Rapiers!
Stilettos! Letter knives used to open
linen envelopes, 19 stories above the
upper West Side.

Well what about us and our razors?
*The Rhythms, The Chicago Nation,
The Crescent Moons, The Pythons* or
The Berkeley Boppers? Man, we
Dukes and do we? Muhammad Ali rum
blers; Riders of the Purple Rage

Dear *Atlantic Monthly* Dec. 1970.
Is Augustus still the Emperor? Can
Rev. Billy Moyers dance on a dime?
Is that Ralph Ellison in Frank Sin-
atra's raincoat or Floyd Patterson
lifting several White Hopes from
the canvas? The album notes for
Strangers in the Night?

Well what did I expect? The multi
ple assassin theory of the *L.A.
Free Press*? *E.V.O.*'s hepatitis
yellow? The Dubious Achievements of
Esquire? The Schwarz is Beautiful
school teacher over at *Evergreen*
clinging to her English text?

You pays your dollar and you gets
Tabbed. Ah, that smooth velvet taste
We've come a long way from *Sneaky
Pete*, now hain't we? You know
we is

Confidentially though,
a young writer informed me that
this *Atlantic* issue made him
feel like Sugar Ray among the
Mormons. The black-as-Ham Utah
night when Sugar took off Gene
Fullmer's jaw. Never will for
get it. A left hook from out
of nowhere. And before his crafty
handlers could wise their boy to
the Sean O Casey shuffle and the
Mark Twain Possum, Fullmer had
done received his Baron Saturday
and was out cold on the floor.

"Why did they stop it? I'm not
hurt, the Kayoed Kid complain
ed. But it was too late, the sta
dium was empty, and Sugar was
on the train.

The Last Week in 30

FOR VICTOR CRUZ ON D MOON

5 before 2/22 i am
a magnified lizard in
a science fiction film. 1944
is when it was made; the
year ol men played volley
ball w/ children before add
ing them to the bones of
       europe

mother of dragons a swell
head said just as the ufo
carried him off. right
on time too; they signed his
happy papers d day befo. he
couldn/t keep his tongue
       still

i am spending my birthday in
a city built on junk left by
    a   glacier

a zoology professor/s wife jumped
off a bridge last week. that
fri he heard heavy breathing on
the other end of the line. the
news called it alienation

aint gon kill this cat. i
am moving into a new age. today
i broke the ice. my pulse begins to
move across a new world.

Loup Garou Means Change Into

If Loup Garou means change into
When will I banish mine?
I say, if Loup Garou means change
Into when will I shed mine?
This eager Beast inside of me
Seems never satisfied

I was driving on the Nimitz wasn't
Paying it no mind
I was driving on the Nimitz wasn't
Paying it no mind
Before you could say "Mr. 5 by 5"
I was doin 99

My Cherokee is crazy
Can't drink no more than 4
My Cherokee is crazy
Can't stand no more than 4
By the time I had my 15th one
I was whooping across the floor
I was talking whiskey talking
I was whooping across the floor

Well, I whistled at a Gypsy who was reading at my cards
She was looking at my glad hand when something came
Across the yard started wafting across the kitchen
Started drifting in the room, the black went out her
Eyeballs a cat sprung cross her tomb
I couldn't know what happened till I looked behind the door
Where I saw her cold pale husband
WHO'S BEEN DEAD SINCE 44

They say if you get your 30
You can get your 35
Folks say if you get to 30
You can make it to 35
The only stipulation is you
Leave your Beast outside

Loup Garou the violent one
When will you lay off me
Loup Garou the Evil one
Release my heart my seed
Your storm has come too many times
And yanked me to your sea

I said please Mr. Loup Garou
When will you drop my goat
I said mercy Mr. Loup Garou
Please give me victory
I put out the beans that evening
Next morning I was free

.05

If i had a nickel
For all the women who've
Rejected me in my life
I would be the head of the
World Bank with a flunkie
To hold my derby as i
Prepared to fly chartered
Jet to sign a check
Giving India a new lease
On life

If i had a nickel for
All the women who've loved
Me in my life i would be
The World Bank's assistant
Janitor and wouldn't need
To wear a derby
All i'd think about would
Be going home

The Author Reflects on His 35th Birthday

35? I have been looking forward
To you for many years now
So much so that
I feel you and I are old
Friends and so on this day, 35
I propose a toast to
Me and You
35? From this day on
I swear before the bountiful
Osiris that
If I ever
If I EVER
Try to bring out the
Best in folks again I
Want somebody to take me
Outside and kick me up and
Down the sidewalk or
Sit me in a corner with a
Funnel on my head

Make me as hard as a rock
35, like the fellow in
The story about the
Big one that got away
Let me laugh my head off
With Moby Dick as we reminisce
About them suckers who went
Down with the *Pequod*
35? I ain't been mean enough
Make me real real mean

Mean as old Marie rolling her eyes
Mean as the town Bessie sings about
"Where all the birds sing bass"

35? Make me Tennessee mean
Cobra mean
Cuckoo mean
Injun mean
Dracula mean
Beethovenian-brows mean
Miles Davis mean
Don't-offer-assistance-when
Quicksand-is-tugging-some-poor
Dope-under-mean
Pawnbroker mean
Pharaoh mean
That's it, 35
Make me Pharaoh mean
Mean as can be
Mean as the dickens
Meaner than mean

When I walk down the street
I want them to whisper
There goes Mr. Mean
"He's double mean
He even turned the skeletons
In his closet out into
The cold"

And 35?
Don't let me trust anybody
Over Reed but
Just in case
Put a tail on that
Negro too
                              February 22, 1973

Jacket Notes

Being a colored poet
Is like going over
Niagara Falls in a
Barrel

An 8 year old can do what
You do unaided

The barrel maker doesn't
Think you can cut it

The gawkers on the bridge
Hope you fall on your
Face

The tourist bus full of
Paying customers broke-down
Just out of Buffalo

Some would rather dig
The postcards than
Catch your act

A mile from the brink
It begins to storm

But what really hurts is
You're bigger than the
Barrel

A Secretary to the Spirits

Pocadonia

You dragged me into your love pond
Pocadonia, your snapping turtle got the
best of me
You dragged me into your love pond
Pocadonia, your snapping turtle got
the best of me
It was raining down on Hang-over morning
my head was in a sag
I looked over at your pillow
A crease was where you used to be

For one whole year after you left
I wouldn't hardly touch my food
For one skinny year after you left
I wouldn't hardly touch my food
lived on wheat chex and peanut butter
lived on crusty bread and rice

Slept on a cold cold floor for a mattress
Dressed in salt water crocodile skin
Slept on a cold cold floor for a mattress
Dressed in salt water crocodile skin
People would point at me and murmur
Whenever I'd leave my den

Caught catfish with my barehands
And breaded it Cedar Rapids style
Caught catfish with my barehands
and fried it Cedar Rapids style
My only form of diversion
Was the hoot owls who were hooting outside

Used to go up on Indian Mountain
Watch the Gold Coast ships come in
Used to go up on Indian Mountain
Watch the Gold Coast ships come in
Wondering where was my red-eyed Pocadonia
Wondering where was my baby's been

I see by the Magnavox
where they burn candles for you
on the beaches of Rio
Images of you on the finest pottery
All the school girls wear the shampoo
you wear
Your face on the national stamps like
the King's
The drunk plays your song on the
Seabird till three
Pocadonia, Pocadonia why have you
forgotten me?

You up there on television
doing your standard trance dance
the thirty-foot Indian Python
the one I gave you resting on
your shoulders like white wings
They done made you Ms. Spirit World

Pocadonia Pocadonia
Do you remember me?
As you ride next to your new Obeah
Three finger Jack of the Bugaboo trade
In his 1971 white Eldorado, eyes behind shades
Wearer of imitation leopard skin suits
He's made you his slave
He has a franchise on wing-tipped shoes
He's done turned your eye again

His rhythm section sounds like beer cans
Rattling from the rear of a wedding hearse
You always like them loud Pocadonia
Your bent for plaid men with their lucky Roots

Rabbit's foot $300.00 leather-pants skin tight
They love to show out at ringside
During the Ali-Frazier fight
Pocadonia, you have gone red on me again

Pocadonia, my love do you remember me
When they duppy you again please don't
Call on me
I'm like a full-up motel with a fabulous view
My dreams, they say, No Vacancy to you
I'm like a full-up motel with a fabulous view
My dreams, they say, No Vacancy to you

*Poem Delivered Before Assembly of Colored
People Held at Glide Memorial Church,
Oct. 4, 1973 and Called to Protest Recent
Events in the Sovereign Republic of Chile*

In the winter of 1966 Pablo Neruda
Lifted 195 lbs of ragged scrawls
That wanted to be a poet and put
Me in the picture where we stood
Laughing like school chums

No little man ever lifted me like that

Pablo Neruda was a big man
It is impossible for me to believe that
Cancer could waste him
He was filled with barrel-chested poetry
From stocky head to feet and
Had no need for mortal organs
The cancer wasn't inside of Pablo Neruda
Cancer won't go near poetry
The cancer was inside ITT
The Cancer God with the
Nose of President Waterbugger
The tight-Baptist lips of John Foster Dulles
And the fleshy Q Ball head of
Melvin Laird
Dick Tracy's last victim

The Cancer God with the body
Of the rat-sucking Indian Plague Flea
All creepy transparent and hunched up
Stalks the South American copper
Country with its pet anaconda
It breathes and hollers like

All the Japanese sci fi monsters
Rolled into one: Hogzilla
Its excrescency supply the Portuguese
With napalm

The Cancer God is a bully who mooches up
Rational gentle and humanistic men
But when it picked a fight with the poet
It got all the cobalt-blue words it could use
And reels about holding in its insides

Do something about my wounded mother
Says President Waterbugger
Shambling across the San Clemente beach
Whose sand is skulls grinded
Do something about my wounded mother
Says the slobbering tacky thing
Pausing long enough from his hobby
Ripping-off the eggs of the world
Their albumen oozing down his American
Flag lapel, his bareassed elephant
Gyrating its dung-wings
Give her all of South America if she wants it
And if she makes a mess
Get somebody to clean it up
Somebody dumb
A colonel who holds his inaugural address
Upside down and sports
Miss-matched socks

And if they can't stomach their
New leaders' uglysucker French
Angel faces then cover them up with
A uniform or hide its Most Disgusting
In a tank
Cover it up like they want to cover
Me up those pitiful eyes gazing from
The palm tree freeway of the Dead War

President Waterbugger your crimes
Will not leave office
No imperial plastic surgeon can
Remove them from your face
They enter the bedroom of your
Hacienda at night and rob you
Of your sleep
They call out your name

President Waterbugger
Next to you Hitler resembles
A kindergarten aide
Who only wanted to raise some geese
And cried when listening to
Dietrich Fischer-Dieskau
Everything you put your paws on
Becomes all crummy and yukky
In New Jersey the mob cries for Jumboburgers
In Florida the old people are stealing Vitamin E

President Waterbugger only your crimes
Want to be near you now
Your daughters have moved out of town
Your wife refuses to hold your hand
On the elevator
Inexplicably, Lincoln's picture
Just fell from the wall
Next time you kill a poet
You'd better read his poems first
Or they will rise up and surround you
Like 1945 fire cannons a few miles from
Berlin
And History will find no trace of
Your ashes in the bunker of your hell

A Secretary to the Spirits

The following minutes were
logged by this Secretary to
the Spirits during the last five
years which have occasionally been
like a devil woman on a heart

Sometimes I felt
only a beetle could inch up
from this situation
Y'awl know what I mean

I am no beetle
not even a bishop
got 90% wrong on the priest's
exam
Scared of snakes

Just a red baboon with the
hurricane's eye
got up sometimes in a Businessman's
three-piece
Mostly an errand boy for the spirits
It's honest Work
You can even come by promotions
I'll rise or
maybe grow up even

I hail from a long line of
risers
like Grand ma ma, old oak
off on a new path
she sculpts from the clay

Sather Tower Mystery

Seems there was this Professor
a member of what should be called
The Good German Department

Must have signed his name to
5,000 petitions in front of
the Co-Op on Cedar
and bought two tons of benefit
cookies
Blames Texas for the sorry
state of the oceans
Rode a Greyhound bus "Civil
Rights," Alabama, 1960
Found the long yellow war
"deplorable"
Believes John "Duke" Wayne's
values to be inferior to his

He said, "Ishmael, I'd
love to do the right thing
for as you know I'm all for
the right thing and against
the wrong thing, but
these plaster of paris busts
of deceased Europeans
Our secret ways
Our sacred fears

"These books, leather-bound
'copyright 1789'
All of these things, precious
to me, gleaming like the
stainless steel coffee urn in
the faculty club, an original
Maybeck, 1902

"I'd stand up for Camelot
by golly, even if it meant
shooting all the infidels in
the world," he said
reaching into his desk drawer

"Why, I might even have to
shoot you, Ishmael"

Staring down the cold
tunnel of a hard .38
I thought

*Most people are to the right
when it comes to where they must
eat and lay their heads!*

Foolology

Shaken by his bad press, the wolf
presses north, leaving caribou to
the fox,
Raven, the snow player gets his
before buzzards with bright red
collars move in to dine near the
bottom of a long scavenger line

This poem is about a skunk, no
rather about a man, who though
not of the skunk family uses
his round-eye the way skunks do

After he eats, his friends eat
He is a fool and his friends are
fools but sometimes it's hard to
tell who is the biggest fool this
fool or his fool friends

By the time they catch us
we're not there
We crows
Nobody's ever seen a dead crow
on the highway

First moral: Don't do business
with people for whom April first
is an important date
they will use your bank balance to
buy eight thousand pies, tunics,
ballet slippers with bells and
a mail order lake in the middle of
a desert for splash parties

Second moral: Before you can spot the
fools in others you must rid yourself
of the fool in you
You can tell a fool by his big mouth

The Return of Julian the Apostate to Rome

Julian
Come back
It can't be long
For the emperor

He sees plots everywhere
Has executed three postmen
Rants in print against his
Former allies
Imagines himself a
Yoruba god
Has asked the Bishops to
Deify him

Not only is he short
He's nuts

Julian come back
The people are crapping
In the temples
Barbarian professors
Are teaching one god
They are ripping the limbs
Off our fetishes
They are carving the sea
Monsters from our totems
They made a pile of our
Wood sculpture and set fire
To it

Julian
Come back
Rude hags
Have crashed the senate
And are spitting on the
Elders

Meanwhile, Julian
The perennial art major
Ponders in the right wing
Of the monastery museum

The Egyptian collection

Sputin

Like Venus
My spin is retrograde
A rebel in more ways than one

I click my heels
In seedy taverns
& pinch the barmaids
On the cheeks

Madeira drips from
My devilish beard
My eyes sparkle dart
Flicker & sear
Man, do I love to dance

Something tells me the
Tzar will summon me to
Save his imperial hide

I peeped his messenger
Speeding through the gates of
The Winter Palace

He's heading this way

Soon, my fellow peasants will
See me in the Gazette
Taking tea with the royal family

They'll say
That crazy bum?

Sky Diving

"It's a good way to live and
A good way to die"
From a Frankenheimer video about
Sky diving
The hero telling why he liked to

     The following noon he leaped
     But his parachute wasn't with him
     He spread out on the field like
     Scrambled eggs

Life is not always
Hi-lifing inside
Archibald Motley's
"Chicken Shack"
You in your derby
Your honey in her beret
Styling before a small vintage
Car

Like too many of us
I am a man who never had much
Use for a real father
And so when I'm heading
For a crash
No one will catch me but
Me

The year is only five days old
Already a comet has glittered out
Its glow sandbagged by
The jealous sun

Happens to the best of us
Our brilliance falling off
Like hair from Berkeley's roving
Dogs

Even on Rose Bowl day
An otherwise joyous occasion
A float veered into the crowd
Somebody got bruised over the incident
Like a love affair on second ave.

It's a good lesson to us all
In these downhill days of a
Hard-hearted decade
Jetting through the world
Our tails on fire

You can't always count
On things opening up for you
Know when to let go
Learn how to fall

Soul Proprietorship

I.
Billy Eckstine, now I
understand why you
went solo, even if it meant crooning
the Pastrami and Rye circuit from
Miami to Grossinger's
Maybe you got tired of babysitting
for other people's tubas, or
running out for reeds
Maybe you got tired of the
spitballs breaking the skin
of your neck while in the midst
of one of those ostentatious supper-
club bows
The bounced checks and half-empty
seats were hard on your dignity
and the bad publicity you received
from the black eye you gave your
agent, co-hort in a secret
deal with management
didn't help

II.
You always had to put ice packs
on the lead tenor's head in Chicago
when by late afternoon a concert
was scheduled for Detroit
And there was always the genius
He was avant garde
which meant he had trouble playing
in scales of five flats
he spurned your attempts to

teach him things and went out
to organize his own band
They called their bloopers "new
music" and drew "experimental"
customers

customers who never smiled
and owned high blood pressure
When you travel single you
can take time out to catch up
with the funnies
You no longer have to order
40 cups of coffee
10 black
5 with cream, and
12 regular
You no longer have to keep
tabs on the two guys who wanted
tea

III.
And when your only companion became
your thought
You came up with the Billy Eckstine
Shirt
With prints as beautiful as
the handle of an Islamic sword
and you made a million silver dollars
And you bought an old Spanish mansion
in California whose
wings could be seen from the sea
They look like two shining silver
collars, billowing, for lift off

Vamp

No wonder the vampire
Is dead
From the hem of his
Cloak to the roots of
His fangs he is one big
Dummy

Doesn't he
Know that creeping
Through the open windows
Of people's lives can
Lead to his extinction?
Carrying off peoples'
Dear ones can get him stuck

You can't even
Stake the stud without
Becoming caked in his
Blood

There is a vampire
Who is cutting into
My orderly progression
In my profession
He shadows me about the
Country like an itinerant
Snake
Everything I do, It do

He converts my
Friends into his concoctions
And convinces peasants that
I am their devil
He is putting ignorant
Heat on me

A wicked trick is dying
For me to use it
I can't hold out much longer
Vampire
In my sleep I hear you screaming
Vamp

Wise up Blood Sucker
Or you will have the
Dawn you hate

Sixth Street Corporate War

Not all rats live in sewers
Some of them dwell in 100,000 dollar
rat's nests on the Alameda
and drive to work in a Mercedes
laboratory rat white
You wouldn't even know they were
rats
on the mailbox it says Mr. Rodent

As big as a coffee table book
(The only book in the house)
he spends his time nibbling ratboy
in a rathouse with its
cheesy rat kitchen or scampering
on a rat sofa or in a bed of
rats
Or you might find him at the Ratskeller
wetting his rat whiskers on
rat soup
"my favorite drink" said
This shareholder rat there he
go old bureaucratic rat investor
in rattraps where people live
like rats

As years went by he gained more
status until he became the esteemed
Doctor Rattus
Crashed a tomcat convention and
demanded to be put on the
banquet
This even woke up Scrounger

or Mr. All Claws,
the toastmaster tomcat
catnapping on the dais
after a night of pre-
convention howling
"whaddya say, boys"
said the thrice decorated
rat scrapper
"rat cocktail
rat of the day
rat a la carte
or rat mousse?"

The other cats being
democrats cast their
votes by secret ballot
gulp!

Poetry Makes Rhythm in Philosophy

Maybe it was the Bichot
Beaujolais, 1970
But in an a.m. upstairs on
Crescent Ave. I had a conversation
with K.C. Bird

    We were discussing
rhythm and I said
"Rhythm makes everything move
the seasons swing
it backs up the elements
Like walking Paul-Chamber's fingers"

    "My worthy constituent"
Bird said, "The Universe is a
spiralling Big Band in a
polka-dotted speakeasy,
effusively generating new light
every one-night stand"

We agreed that nature can't
do without rhythm but rhythm can
get along without nature

This rhythm, a stylized Spring
conducted by a blue-collared man
in Keds and denims
(His Williamsville swimming pool
shaped like a bass clef)
in Baird Hall
on Sunday afternoons
Admission Free!

All *harrumphs!* must be
checked in at
the door

I wanted to spin
Bennie Moten's
"It's Hard to Laugh or Smile"
but the reject wouldn't automate
and the changer refused to drop
"Progress," you know

Just as well
because Bird vanished

A steel band had
entered the room

Untitled

Today I feel bearish
I've just climbed out of
A stream with a jerking
Trout in my paw

Anyone who messes with
Me today will be hugged
And dispatched

The Reactionary Poet

If you are a revolutionary
Then I must be a reactionary
For if you stand for the future
I have no choice but to
Be with the past

Bring back suspenders!
Bring back Mom!
Homemade ice cream
Picnics in the park
Flagpole sitting
Straw hats
Rent parties
Corn liquor
The banjo
Georgia quilts
Krazy Kat
Restock

The syncopation of
Fletcher Henderson
The Kiplingesque lines
of James Weldon Johnson
Black Eagle
Mickey Mouse
The Bach Family
Sunday School
Even Mayor La Guardia
Who read the comics
Is more appealing than
Your version of
What Lies Ahead

In your world of
Tomorrow Humor
Will be locked up and
The key thrown away
The public address system
Will pound out headaches
All day
Everybody will wear the same
Funny caps
And the same funny jackets
Enchantment will be found
Expendable, charm, a
Luxury
Love and kisses
A crime against the state
Duke Ellington will be
Ordered to write more marches
"For the people," naturally

If you are what's coming
I must be what's going

Make it by steamboat
I likes to take it real slow

Rough Trade Slumlord Totem

Here's how you put your enemy
atop a totem where the scavengers
get at him

This is for you, dummy
who hoarded our writings in
your basement, four solid months
like your brother landlord of
Sitka, Alaska, who chopped-up
the Tlingit totems for bar-b-cue chairs

The Raven will get you sucker
The Raven will hunt you down
Gaaaaaa! Gaaaaaaa! sucker

The thunder will empty its
bladder on your face you
seal-cow man who wobbles on
his belly with common
law fish in his mouth

May seagulls litter your
Punch-and-Judy corked eyes
May the eagle mistake your
snout for a mouse and sink
its claws into it
May the paint used on your
head be slum lord paint bound
to peel in a short time

And when you crash I hope
your landing place be
a maggot's hunting party
And while the rest of the
totem journey's into mother
soil
your segment remains
your sideshow providing
Laughing Forest
with a belly full

Tea Dancer Turns Thirty-nine

They will swoon no more his
four o'clock afternoons,
He bids farewell to his taxi
dancing heart throbs
He donates his clicks to the
Boogie Hall of Fame
Roll on Mississippi Roll on

From Beyond, cognac-voiced
Bojangles sent him El Rito
strawberries covered with Jack
Frost sugar, big as peaches!

A gesture from a man who could
Essence so, God ringed Satan to
wish him Happy Birthday

　　　Not too far back
his silver medals danced in
the brightest hock windows of
Bret Harte Boardwalk.
Now, it's caviar omelettes at
number one Fifth Ave

What changed his luck?

The little lady he calls his
Tiger Balm, the one beneath a Coit
Tower, half way up from Half Moon
Bay?

He hurries to her
Her red dragon in his eyes
red as the red trees of Modesto
red as the red in the red bridge of
death
Moon Ocean red

Colorwheels light upon Filipino gazers
in the Palace of Old Tokyo town their
wriggling rumps rooting for Donald Byrd
and the Black Byrds while just across town
romance has been replaced by shrunken jeans
You look like a sack, he said, before she
hurled chocolate milk at his white
European double-breasted suit

An embarrassing situation for the Order
of the Golden Bear, on the other side
of the Bay Bridge, having to negotiate
with lucky Feet who tripped them up
like the accidental hero in the Bank Dick
He spilled ashes all over the Queen's
Thug rug
She could do nothing but smile her
Silver-Jubilee smile, an outrage
to the civilized world
Would your majesty jern me in a game
of chanct? he said, sweeping his big
hairy floor-length arms and flipping
drumsticks to the ceiling
Will crocodiles reach Kampala this
year, or the Taj Mahal yellow?

They laughed at his blue serge suit
Dobbs crumpled from being sat on
but when he fired a revolver into
the cushion, they knew he wasn't
kidding

And then there was the
Tea Dancer's march when the old ones
put the young set to shame with their
glides, kneebends, squats and
twirls

These days you have to have a Ph.D.
In the old days all you had to do was
dance

We mount our old days next to our stuffed
shoes and feed them wines only popes used
to drink

He's a spin around fool and his eyes are
kind of hazy but that don't mean he's lazy
if anything it means he's crazy
Give him a thousand dollars and he'll
sign off his professional frog's legs
(a minute of silence for Legs Diamond,
tea dancer, slain in Niagara Falls phone
booth—most people run out of steam—
tea dancers run out of dimes)

He doesn't know the difference between
his golden slippers and Stacey Adams
continued Fast Foods, the Boss
I ought to know, I run a factory full
of dead horses
when I'm not killing television

He thought of what Leslie Laguna said
in the Hotel Loretto up near Santa
Fe way, about why hares are heroines
in trickster tales
Because they're quick! she said
The Quick and the Dead

And so from the Papyrus Room
of the Pyramid Hotel
high above the River Nile of
his dream
Let's spin out some to
a crackling bundle
of Tennessee two-fisted
aqua-eyed fire
Born in grand old Oakland
on the day of six twos
Her smile spanned the delivery room

Finally, this item
today is the seventh
day of the seventh month
of the seventy-seventh year
of this century

Apples grow on trees!

Points of View

For Dancer

When lovers die they blossom
grapes
That's why there's so much
wine in love
That's why I'm still drunk
on you

Earthquake Blues

Well the cat started actin funny
and the dog howled all night long
I say the cat started actin very frightful
and the birds chirped all night long
The ground began to rumble
As the panic hit the town.

Mr. Earthquake Mr. Earthquake
you don't know good from bad
Mr. Earthquake Mr. Earthquake
you don't know good from bad
You kill the little child in its nursery
You burn up the widow's pad

The buildings started swaying
like a drunk man walking home
The buildings started swaying
like a drunk man walking home
The people they were running
and the hurt folks began to moan

Mr. Earthquake Mr. Earthquake
you don't know good from bad
Mr. Earthquake Mr. Earthquake
you don't know good from bad
You kill the little child in its nursery
You burn up the widow's pad

I got underneath my table
Had my head between my knees
I got underneath the table
Had my head between my knees
The dishes they were rattlin
and the house was rockin me

Mr. Earthquake Mr. Earthquake
you don't know good from bad
Mr. Earthquake Mr. Earthquake
you don't know good from bad
You kill the little child in its nursery
You burn up the widow's pad

I was worried about my baby
Was she safe or was she dead
I was worried about my baby
Was she safe or was she dead
When she phoned and said I'm
ok, Daddy. Then I went on back
to bed.

Mr. Earthquake Mr. Earthquake
you don't know good from bad
Mr. Earthquake Mr. Earthquake
you don't know good from bad
You kill the little child in its nursery
You burn up the widow's pad

Points of View

I

The pioneer stands in front of the
Old pioneer's home with his back-pack
walking stick and rifle
Wasn't me that Kisadi Frog-Klan
Indian was talking about when he
mentioned the horrors of Alaska
What horrors of Alaska?
Why Baranof was a swell fellow
Generous to the Indians, he was
known as far south as California
for his good deeds
Before we came the Indians were
making love to their children and
sacrificing their slaves, because
the Raven told them so, according
to them
"They couldn't even speak good
English and called the streams and
the mountains funny names
They were giving each other refrigerators
the potlatches had become so bad

We made them stop
They'd build a canoe abandon
it, then build another
We made them stop that, too
Now they have lawyers

They can have anything they want
If they want to go whaling
when we know they don't need to
go whaling
The lawyers see to it that they
go whaling
They're just like us
They buy frozen snow peas
just like we do
They're crazy about motorcycles
Just like we are

We brought them civilization
We brought them penicillin
We brought them Johnny Carson
Softball
We brought them trailer camps
They'd get married at fourteen
and die at 24
We brought them longevity

II
They brought us carbon dioxide
They brought us contractors
We told them not to dig there
They were clawed by two eagles
While uncovering the graves of
two medicine men

The white man has the mind of a
walrus's malignant left ball
We don't think the way they do
They arrive at the rate of one
thousand per month in cars
whose license plates read
texas oklahoma and mississippi
They built the Sheffield Hotel on
a herring bed
Everywhere are their dogs
Everywhere are their guns
Everywhere are their salmon-faced

women who get knocked up a lot
and sometimes enter the Chanel
restaurant wearing mysterious black
eyes, socked into their Viking-eyes
by men whose hair is plastered with
seal dung
It all began when
Chief Kowee of the Raven Klan showed
Joe Juneau the location of the gold
Now Mount Juneau is as empty as
a box of popcorn on the floor of
a picture show
When our people saw the first
Russian ship, we thought it was
the White Raven's return
Instead it was the Czarina's pirate
Dressed in Russian merchant's clothes
and a peacock's hat.
He shot Katlian in the back

The Ballad of Charlie James

I
Hunter's Point: Night
Papa Charlie James awakes
to see the 'Frisco police
at the foot of his bed
"Bring them hands from
underneath them sheets so's
we can see them. Let us see
what you got beneath those
sheets," they said, shooting
seventeen rounds of ammunition
into Charlie's bed

II
He survived the crazy rhythms
in his chest
his lungs whistling like
ghost winds, but he couldn't
survive the police
Hazardous to your health
if you are poor, Indian, or
Chicano, or if you're a sixty
year old black man asleep in
bed "Bring them hands from
underneath those sheets so's we can
see them, let us see what you got
beneath those sheets"

Like in Count Albuquerque's
town, where underneath the freeway
a lone woman wears "I Want Your Body"
on her t-shirt, a black man can get

shot for just horsing around
They use the redman for target
practice, they hang the Mexican
in jail.
O ain't it a shame what they did
to poor Charlie James. Have mercy
and ain't it a shame
"He just played dominoes
drank soda water, and looked
out the window" his neighbors said
Thinking of his poor wife in a
Georgia loony bin
she saw her children die
one by one
Thinking of his mother out
there in the backwater cemetery
her shroud faded
her eye sockets, windows for
spiders, "Bring them hands
from underneath those sheets so's
we can see them. Let us see what you
have beneath those sheets"
The sign on Charlie's door
"Making Love Is Good For You"
shot full of bulletholes

His brains liver and kidneys
gone up in smoke
"Making Love Is Good For You"
His stomach will hold no more
beans
no more bad coffee
his lips have seen their last
cigarette
O ain't it a shame what they did
To Charlie James. Have mercy ain't
it a shame.

They said his homicide was justified
the parrot D.A. "concurred"
The police were just doing their
duty, they said, and the
parrot D.A. "concurred, concurred"
O the parrot D.A. "concurred"
O ain't it a shame what they did
to poor Charlie James
"Making Love Is Good For You"
"Bring them hands from underneath
those sheets so's we can see them.
Let's see what you have beneath those
sheets."

Points of View

The pioneers and the indians
disagree about a lot of things
for example, the pioneer says that
when you meet a bear in the woods
you should yell at him and if that
doesn't work, you should fell him
The indians say that you should
whisper to him softly and call him by
loving nicknames
No one's bothered to ask the bear
what he thinks

Bitch

When's the last time you
saw a dog eat a dog

When men invented the term
Bitch
They were talking about
themselves

Datsun's Death

"Down in Puerto Rico, when
we didn't have no kerosene
we used the stuff to read by"
the stuff
he took his first drink
at twenty, and by the age of
40 had sauced up enough to fill
all the billboard bottles from
Lafitte's Galveston to Houston's
Texas
There's enough light in his belly
to fire all the gas lamps in
Cincinnati
He remembers getting burned in Cincinnati
his radiator was hot
his temperature was rising
like the white 68 Dodge grumbling
up Moeser Lane, as ferocious as a
pit-bull
The accident cop would later
say
It must have been built like a
tank
rammed into my piece of tail
a hit and run, you've been there
haven't you partner
haven't you?

It was A.T. and T. which reminded us
that the heaviest traffic occurs at
4:30 a.m.
All the phone circuits are busy

I loves you baby
You know i loves you baby!
Do you loves me baby?
I don't care what you women
say
Prometheus was a man
the X rays just came back
his liver looks terrible

For the ground crew
at the Kirksville
airport a sweetheart
is the otter jetstream
of Illinois Airlines
while the two-toned
Monte Carlo parked next
to the Robin breasted
cornfield is baby

For me heaven was
tooling around in the
driver's seat of my
280ZX
my honey of the midnight blue
my import car of the year
mutilated by the brazen chrome
of a snorting bull-car
hot and swerving under
the El Cerrito moon

Plymouth, Cadillac, Mercury
Montego, the automobile gods
rattled in their Richmond junkyards
Chrysler and Ford sales went down
30% the next day
And the shining new sacrifices on display
at banner-waving San Bruno
parking lots,
Wept from their windshields
Some used-up like my Datsun
Head mashed against the rhododendrons

On the Fourth of July in Sitka, 1982

On the fourth of July in Sitka
Filipinos sold shish-ka-bob from their
booths in the park
On the fourth of July in Sitka, the children
dressed in deerskin jackets
and coonskin caps
On the fourth of July in Sitka, you
could buy fishpie in the basement of St. Michael's
Church, where the vodka-drunken Russians used to
pray
But the red white and blue cake was not for sale

On the fourth of July in Sitka the people
kicked off shoes and ran through the
streets, pushing beds
On the fourth of July in Sitka, tour buses
with yellow snouts and square heads
delivered tourists to the Shee Atika lodge
where they stared at floats designed by
Sheldon Jackson College and
the Alaska Women in Timber
On the fourth of July in Sitka the
Gajaa Heen dancers performed, wearing their
Klan emblems of Beaver Wolf Killer Whale
Porpoise, and Dog Salmon

On the fourth of July in Sitka the Libertarian
Party announced the winners of its five dollar raffle
1st Prize, a Winchester .300 Magnum
2nd Prize, an Ithaca 12 gauge shotgun
3rd Prize, a Sportsman III knife

On the fourth of July in Sitka the
softball teams were honored at the American
Legion Club and the players drank champagne till dawn
On the fourth of July in Sitka, the night was
speckled with Japanese fireworks
sponsored by Alaska Lumber and Pulp

On the fifth of July in Sitka
a Canadian destroyer brought to Sitka
for the fourth of July in Sitka sailed
through Sitka Sound and out into the
Northern Pacific
All of the men on board stood at
attention, saluting their audience
three bald eagles, two ravens, and me
watching the whole show from Davidoff Hill
the fifth of July in Sitka

Petite Kid Everett

The bantamweight King of
Newark
He couldn't box
He couldn't dance
He just kept coming at
you, glass chin first
Taking five punches for
every one he connected with
you

Petite Kid Everett
He missed a lot
Slipped a lot and
By mid-life he'd
developed one heck
of a sorehead
Took to fighting in
the alley
Gave up wearing a mouthpiece
Beat up his trainers
Beat up the referee
Beat up his fans
Beat up everybody who was
in his corner
Even jumped on Houston Jr.
the lame pail boy
Who didn't have good sense

Petite Kid Everett
There's talk of a comeback
He's got new backers
He stands on one of the four
corners, near the Prudential Life
Building
Trading blows with ghosts
Don't it make you wanna cry?

Turning Pro

There are just so many years
you can play amateur baseball
without turning pro
All of a sudden you realize
you're ten years older than
everybody in the dugout
and that the shortstop could
be your son

The front office complains
about your slowness in making
the line-up
They send down memos about
your faulty bunts and point out
how the runners are always faking
you out
"His ability to steal bases
has faded" they say
They say they can't convince
the accountant that there's such
a thing as "Old Time's Sake"
But just as the scribes were
beginning to write you
off
as a has-been on his last leg
You pulled out that fateful
shut-out
and the whistles went off
and the fireworks scorched a
747
And your name lit up the scoreboard
and the fans carried you on their
shoulders right out of the stadium
and into the majors

Epistolary Monologue

My Dearest Michael:

My favorite lady-in-waiting is so loyal. She certainly can keep a secret. Every day at teatime she sneaks me three bottles of Beefeater. She knows that I can't stand tea. Today she brought me your note. This morning, she had to bring me two tablets of Myaatal. I still haven't recovered from my trip to America. Must have been the tacos and beans we ate at the Reagan's Ranch. That woman is so rude. You remember how she tried to upstage me during her trip to London? Wailing about town with her motorcycle escorts. Got up in that tacky red dress and those wide-brimmed hats that make her resemble a witch. I was speaking to her husband, and the poor man fell asleep. Still telling the same jokes.

But back to your note, my sweet. Michael, I was so touched, but how would it look if another scandal happened to the Windsors? They still haven't gotten over Uncle Edward. If I ran away with you, the public would take away our allowances and evict us from Buckingham Palace. How would we survive? On hotdogs and beans. Our only experience is shaking hands and smiling. And there doesn't seem to be an awful demand for people who know how to walk in processions.

Somebody has to keep a level head. Andrew carrying on with that tart. Diana locked up in her room starving herself, all because she found out Charles's secret. The secret we've kept from the public all these years. Her look-alike is threatening to reveal the whole sordid business if she doesn't receive more money. And Princess Anne. Granted that she is my daughter, but sometimes I think that she's so ugly she should be arrested for public ugliness. The poor young man she's living with is always talking about leaving her. He says that he has to put a bag over her head in order to get a good night's sleep. So please understand, my darling. I do love you. Queens have feelings too, but if I married you, a poor laborer, who would feed my horses and my dogs?

Well, it's 2:00 a.m. here in the Palace. As the Americans say, "I'm in my gin." I just turned off all of the lights. Everyone here is so wasteful. Philip and my bodyguards are in the next room watching videocassettes of "Dynasty" and squealing with delight. O, I wish I could be like that Krystle. Always taking chances, going where her heart leads. But I've grown accustomed to my duty, my position, and the grand tradition of which I am a symbol.

And so, don't be cross with me when my lady-in-waiting delivers this note to you. Goodbye, my darling. And please forgive me for having you arrested. But when we were lying in bed that morning, and you complained about what you would and wouldn't do, I had to put you in your place. Though we were lovers, I was still your sovereign, which meant that my wish was your command.

Love,
Lilibet

Monkey Island

To the monkeys on Monkey Island
the danger signal for man is the
same as that for an approaching
python
That's why the monkeys on Monkey
Island chatter their tails off
when we stand in front of their
cages
They know something that we
Zoo Keepers don't know
Haven't you thought of a person
and said to yourself
that snake

The Pope Replies to the Ayatollah Khomeini

My Dear Khomeini:

I read your fourteen thousand dollar
ad asking me why the Vatican waited
all of these years to send an envoy
to complain about conditions in Iran
You're right, we should have sent one
when the Shah was in power, look,
I'm in total agreement with you
Khomeini, that Christ, had he lived in
Iran under the Shah, would have led the
biggest damned revolt you ever saw

Believe me, Khomeini, I knew about
the Shah's decadence, his extravagance
his misdeeds, and how he lolled about
in luxury with Iran's loot
I knew about the trail of jewels which
led to his Dad's capture
but a fella has to eat and so when
David Rockefeller asked me to do something
how could I refuse?

You can afford to be holier than thou
What is it, 30 dollars per barrel these days?
You must be bathing in oil
While each day I suffer a new indignity

You know that rock record they made me
do? It's 300 on the Charts which is about
as low as you can get.
And I guess you read where I

had to call in all those Cardinals and
for the first time reveal the Vatican
budget?
I had to just about get down on my hands
and knees to get them to co-sign for a
loan
The Vatican jet has a mechanical problem
and the Rolls-Royce needs a new engine
The staff hasn't been paid in months
and the power company is threatening to
turn off the candles
To add to that, the building inspector
has listed us as having 30,000 code
violations
I'm telling you, Khomeini, that
so many people are leaving the church
I have this nightmare where I
wake up one day in Los Angeles and
I'm the only one left

Pretty soon we'll be one of those
cults you read about in the *San
Francisco Chronicle*
And so, Khomeini, I promise
you that when we pay off the
deficit, I won't send an envoy
I'll come visit you myself

I'd like to discuss this plan
that Patriarch Dimitrios, of
the Greek Orthodox Church, and I
just came up with

You know, we haven't spoken to
those fellows in 900 years but
when you are 20 million dollars
in the red
You'll talk to anybody

Inaugural Day, 1981

I feel like a Zulu
spying from a rock while
below, the settlers exchange
toasts on the grounds where
a massacre of the Zulus occurred
They are filthy rich
Their wives are dolled-up in
black mink
There is much hugging and
squealing
These people like
Glenn Miller a whole lot
    52 of their countrymen
have been freed by the barbarians
overseas
    "Just out of the trees. The
Only way I'm going back is in a
B-52," he said, putting some hair
on his chest, and passing around
a jug of whiskey
    The settlers shoot at stars
    The settlers jitterbug all
    night
On the Zulu grounds
I have nine children buried there
nine were all they could find

Mossy

If you want to save some money
Always stare a gift cat in the mouth
Especially if you bought him on
Russian Hill
He might have developed
A palate

Untitled

When California is split in two
The Northern part will be called
The Republic of Jambalaya
The Southern part will be called
Summer Camp

Grizzly

He always prided himself on
never being caught with his paws down
The flying grizzly left his bear
tracks at fifty thousand feet
his life, a daily peach blossom
He always managed to find some
hot honey to dip into
He was smiling all the time
Licking his lips, till Mrs.
Grizzly discovered him in the
bush with some outside trim of
a wonderful red cabbage and Mrs.
Grizzly grounded her
Teddy Bear
the rough rider under her fur coat
she was not taken in by his sweet
word-bees
Last trip back to the cave
he felt like he'd entered customs
after a return from an enemy city
What are these claw marks doing on your back?
Are those huckleberry stains on the front
of your pants?
Why do you have that fishy smell?
The divorce left him belly-up

He's somewhere right now
dressed in white and black
checkered pants
being led at the neck by a rope
While he bangs on a dirty
bass drum
a little monkey toots a whistle
and little dogs taunt him
and little children tug at
his ears

Judas

Funny about best friends
huh, Lord
Always up in your face
laughing and talking
leading the praise after
your miracles
That Judas, you had great
hopes for him
Good background
Good-looking, even in a
corduroy suit, made in
Poland, and thirty dollar
shoes
It was his quiet appeal that
kept the group in wine money

As soon as you turned your
back, he took your business
to the Goyim
Told them you going around
telling everybody you the
son-of-god
See how careful you have to
be about whom you go bar-
hopping with, Jesus

Now you're drowsy, Jesus
They've pricked you full of
Thorazine
They've given you electro-
convulsive therapy

You don't know where you
are
You have sores where the
straight-jacket doesn't fit
You're wringing wet from
where you've been sweatin
all night
You squirm on filthy straw

But stick it out, Jesus
where you're going
the drums don't stop
They serve Napa Valley
champagne at every meal
Everybody smokes big cigars
Sweet Angel hair be tingling
your back while you invent
proverbs in a hot tub

Where Judas is going
the people don't know how
to fix ribs
the biscuits taste like
baking soda
The wine is sweet and sticky
Flowers can't grow on this
landscape of jinxed hearts
the Field of Blood
to this day it's called
the Field of Blood

Dialog Outside the Lakeside Grocery

The grocery had provided him with
boxes of rotten lettuce
He was loading them onto a
yellow pick-up truck
He was a frail white man and
wore a plaid woolen shirt and
frayed dungarees
I was sitting in a gray chevrolet
rent-a-dent
"I have eight adult geese and
twenty-six ducks," he said
and i said
"I'll bet you have a big management
problem," and he said
"They're no trouble at all. My
wife raised two of them in the house.
When she goes near their pen
the geese waddle towards her
and nibble the lettuce out of her
hand"
"I'd never think of killing them"
he said
"They keep me out of the bars"

Invasion

Tough guy
He fondles the public
as though it were a
kissing baby
Playing giddyup with his
Stetson
His wife has this thing about
the color blue
Why is it that when the old
men have power the young men
fly home in star-spangled skins

Beats me
The liars on t.v.
They have turned me against the
head of hair, parted on the left side
Under the eyes of god, at night
They cry into sympathetic bourbon
Casper, the malevolent duppy
Doesn't crack a smile in his
hard pinched face
They bombed the mad house by
accident
A level headed pilot came back
Three times, the nurse testified
"I'll remember his grin for the
rest of my life."

The mad house is located on the
Island of Grenada
It is where they chain the crazy
people

Untitled

Alaska's rape
dismemberment
disassembled piece by piece
and shipped to the lower
forty-eight so that people
in Dallas may own whale-
sized cadillacs and lear
jets which cost Alaska an
arm and a leg just like
ravished Jamaica whose
stolen sugar built Mansfield
Park where idle gang rapers
discuss flower beds and
old furniture
Jamaica, Alaska, sisters
dragged into an alley
used and abandoned

Poem for Two Daughters

Everybody wants to know
Where's your oldest daughter
Her first sentence was
phenomenon
Sixteen years later she
stands before you, drawing
on a cigarette
She says she's found you
out
She has exactly eighty dollars
to her name
she thinks she grown
She says she wants her emancipation
You tell her to spell it
She calls you a nerd, a dork
and other words you hear on the
3:15 Arlington #7 Bus
The Yo-Yo special

We used to chide the sightseeing
middle aged in those days when
we stood on our heads outside the Dom
Now, we are the ones sitting on the
greyline
We cannot figure out what it is
we are staring at

Our stomachs hurt
We gaze from houses with un-
obstructed views of the Bay
thirty years ago we couldn't come
up here
Nowadays the neighbors bring pies

Our daughters are either standing up
for the first time or flying

The youngest one puts everything
into her mouth, pencils, your hair
graham crackers, the cat, the car keys
even the Sesame Street book covered
with blue-fuzzed creatures with
purple noses and egg-shaped eyes
She trounces the trampoline in
the kindergym but's too plump for
the Olympics
Her first sentence was: "I see"

The oldest one, as fast as
Clifford Brown on Cherokee
Of another system, impatient
with your inability to cope with
the basic concepts of her world
grinds you up with her mind
Intellectually shoves you about
like you the
wildest Turkey in the state of
Georgia, guiding the hunters to
your roost
You have to fall back on
"It's so because I say it's so"

The differences between the three
would be revealed if someone were to
ask each what they would do if
the world was offered to them on
a silver platter
The youngest one would say
I'd eat it
or at least jump up and down
on it a few times
The oldest one would strut up and down
in front of the world, scolding the world
about its ancient corruption

She'd fast
By the time the question reached
you
the world would have run out of
bones

Phoebe

Phoebe is the 9th satellite
of Saturn
Phoebe is the moon
bending the golden blades
of El Cerrito
A voice brighter than the
lights of the harness racing
fields
Snow has returned to the Sierras
snow has returned to the Rockies
Mount Shasta of opium-
headed Lemurian ceremony
Altars made of whalebone
five thousand years old
California tumbled into the
Pacific
The Indians wrote:
I am burning for snow
said Mount Diablo

Once, because I missed
the snow I made a yellow
streak to Montpelier, Vermont
to witness a white rainbow
to entwist myself in a white rainbow
my Montpelier, population one
she used to belong to a
fisherman

Untitled

I know of a man who treated his body like a dog
the dog ran away

The Middle Class Blues

MONOLOGUE

I can't believe it's 1994. Back in 84 it meant something, but nowadays being middle class and a nickel won't buy you a cup of coffee. During the rest of the 80s the frig was still full and you could always mambo in Guadalajara during the discount off seasons. But by the beginning of the 90s, the only difference between us and the poor was that everything they owned was on their backs while everything we owned was being lent to us by the banks. The banks were on our backs. I was over my head in billy dues. Me and the Mrs. argued so about money that one day she just upped and left. And these were supposed to be our golden years. Some golden years. I can't seem to save over a couple of hundred dollars and I'm spending a third more than I'm making. It's only a matter of time before I have to visit one of those bankruptcy consultants. Talking about the new poor. Never thought it would happen to me. What happened to the old poor? I dunno. They were kicked out of the bus stations, the parks and the welfare hotels a long time ago. Some say they went South. Others say that the society people had them shipped to Central America because down there they know how to handle the poor. Wherever they are, they must have been desperate. They left behind their blues. I'm lucky I guess. I can still afford a martini.

I

I got the middle class blues
I play by middle class rules
O, this middle class life
Is a life full of strife
The bourgeois state can be
A sweet and sour pill
When the first rolls around
You gotta deal with the bills

So hey, Mr. Bartender,
Bring me a dry vermouth and gin
Fix me a black olive and a big martini
Before I hit the wind

II

I constantly get headaches
And my back is often sore
Being the first one on the freeway
Is becoming such a chore
At work they got a robot
That soon will have my job
I'm too old to start all over
Too old to learn to rob

So hey, Mr. Bartender
Bring me a dry vermouth and gin
Fix me a black olive and a big martini
Before I hit the wind

III

The roof is always leaking
The plumbing needs some screws
Everybody on the block, it seems
Knows how to bar-b-cue
My next door neighbors are ticked at me
My lawn is turning brown
There's always something that must be fixed
Everytime you turn around

Hey, hey, Mr. Bartender
Bring me a dry vermouth and gin
Fix me a black olive and a big martini
Before I hit the wind

IV

My son is getting married
To a woman older than me
He just turned twenty the other
week
She's going on sixty-three

My daughter's on narcotics
Her eyes are always red
The car wouldn't start this morning
And I toss and turn in bed

So hey, Mr. Bartender
Bring me a dry vermouth and gin
Fix me a black olive and a big martini
Before I hit the wind

V

The communists say I'm an ingrate
The capitalists took my house
The old people say I neglect them
The young call me a louse
The tax man sent me a letter
He's coming here tonight
Sometimes it gets so heavy
At home, I'm never right

So hey, Mr. Bartender
Bring me a dry vermouth and gin
Fix me a black olive and a big martini
Before I hit the wind

VI

The Doctor says it's no good
To have this stress and mess
The ulcers that will get you
A classy middle class nest
A cat that won't eat store food
Must have its abalone
And don't forget the deadline
To pay the alimony

So hey, Mr. Bartender
Bring me a dry vermouth and gin
Fix me a black olive and a big martini
Before I hit the wind

VII

Well, I'm tired of paying the dentist
And going under the knife
And doing all the things you do
To stay the bourgeois life
The rich they live in heaven
The poor they live in hell
And I live somewhere in between
A sign outside says for sale

So hey, Mr. Bartender
Bring me a dry vermouth and gin
Fix me a black olive and a big martini
Let me go on get this wind

Oakland Blues

Well it's six o'clock in Oakland
and the sun is full of wine
I say, it's six o'clock in Oakland
and the sun is red with wine
We buried you this morning, baby
in the shadow of a vine

Well, they told you of the sickness
almost eighteen months ago
Yes, they told you of the sickness
almost eighteen months ago
You went down fighting, daddy. Yes
You fought Death toe to toe

O, the egrets fly over Lake Merritt
and the blackbirds roost in trees
O, the egrets fly over Lake Merritt
and the blackbirds roost in trees
Without you little papa
what O, what will become of me

O, it's hard to come home, baby
To a house that's still and stark
O, it's hard to come home, baby
To a house that's still and stark
All I hear is myself
thinking
and footsteps in the dark

Martine's Keen Eyes

"I take them with me to the fights
every night," Martine says
On the top floor of the Chelsea
In a two room, one kitchen apartment
with white walls, Martine lives with
Elvin Jones records and *Paris Match*
and wall to wall boxers, staring out
at you from the blacks and whites of
Martine's keen eyes, and the people
stop by, to tell her how much they
love her pictures, and how they moved
them so: The curly gray-haired black
woman who wanders about New York in a
rent hospital gown, her only friend
a milk-stained overcoat.
The gang members with creole faces,
smiling, in front of a Chevrolet, all
but one, dead within six months
wax-faced in Puerto Rican coffins
bussed by comrades; the sassy
bathing-suited little black girl who
charmed an adoring fire hydrant into
spouting her a lake; the pint-sized
dynamite who spars in front of Martine's
mirrors for hours at a time, and the
Inca-faced four year old who never lost
a fight, in the clubs smelling of pizza
and hotdogs where the fight people drink
beer for hours in the fight clubs
watching the fights

St. Louis Woman

He loves to see that orbed heat collapse behind the white Jefferson arc as the downtown St. Louis sun temples burst

Orange as the inside of a Balaban's lobster they cater in the room of Renoirish Third Reich Speer-room nude portraits where Wash. U. grad student waiters resemble the t.v. crew filming a restaurant scene in "As the World Turns." On a stool outside a black man in little boy's cap and white butcher's coat attracts customers with the gleaming stars of his gold teeth. For four days a storebought apricotheaded St. Louis woman in poor white powder and tobacco-road mascaraed eyelashes told the other waitresses in the Forest Park Hotel to quit putting cream and sugar in his coffee because "He looks spoiled. Big and spoiled."

Daughters of Davy Crockett and Dan Boone with high-Cherokee cheekbones, St. Louis women call closeted plantations with monopoly-board street names, "home" behind fake second empire gates which are locked at night to keep out the townies, Riding bicycles, their eyes buried in the streets, the only blacks wear supermarket names on their t-shirts

They stand on the street's dividing line selling rush hour copies of the St. Louis Post Dispatch like the apple-capped Irish lads in a book about the life and times of Jacob Reiss

They are the last people in the nation who take out their billfolds to show you their relatives and their girlfriends' and boyfriends' relatives and that time they went to Atlantic City

St. Louis is surrounded by ninety municipalities. Only a Filipino with a Harvard M.A. in business can untangle the town, Emile said. Emile said that St. Louis women are dumb blondes who stand you up. Equal rights to them means the right to tantalize but not to put out, Emile said.

"Are you Bruce Lee?" they asked Emile when he landed in Harlem.

Feeling tomorrow and twenty-two, a St. Louis woman told him she could run a whole radio station. She knew where you could fetch a Gucci raincoat for one hundred dollars. In her poetry she is "a black rose." He told her that if her skin really needed a flower why not an African violet to go with her yellow eyes. He told her that her eyes were all the evidence we needed to prove that ancient Asiatics reached Madagascar. He told her that a black rose was common and that she was anything but common and that she was as rare as a white tiger rarely seen in the jungles of India or rare as the image of a white owl carrying off a white ermine in the Bird Book we saw in the museum off Big Bend where we learned that the first words said on the telephone constituted a cry for help.

In the Steinberg auditorium he asked the Dalai Lama's stand in why there were black gods with nigger minstrel white lips and great Nigerian mound noses in Nepalese paintings dated 3,000 B.C.

Before rushing to the next question he said they represented Time. He told the "black rose" that she was as rare as Time hung on a monastery wall, while outside buddhists blow conch horns and chant like a chorus of frogs.

St. Louis women are rabbit-furred hookers who hustle to star wars in the steeple chase room of the chase park hotel where Gorgeous George dressed in sequined Evel Knievel jumpsuit discos to Elvis Presley and the hogged-necked bouncers in blazers threaten to break your arm. There are portraits in that room of horses, skins shining like chestnuts, life-sized statues of jockeys in polka-dotted blouses. The lamps are shaped like racing horns.

St. Louis women write body poetry, play the harp for the symphony and take up archery.

St. Louis women wash cook and clean for St. Louis women who write body poetry, play the harp for the symphony, and take up archery.

A St. Louis woman is the automatic writing hand for a spirit named Ida Mae of the red dress cult who rises from the Mississippi each night to check out the saloons before last call.

She rises from the big river G. Redmond calls Black River, Mike Castro's River Styx, and every body knows about Muddy Waters; St. Louis women are daughters of Episcopalian ministers who couldn't sit still for Grant Wood

Sternly scarfed they stare straight ahead inside Doberman Pinscher station wagons. Their husbands work for McDonnell Douglas, Ralston-Purina, and Anheuser-Busch.

(They still talk about how old man Busch was so rich that when his son killed a man it was the trial judge who served time)

The great grandfather of a St. Louis woman appears in the 100 years of lynching horror book because he owned 300 acres and white men wanted those acres

The grandmother of a St. Louis woman told her that no man can say "I Love You" like a black man. "Velvet be dripping from his lips," a unique experience like the one recounted by a man in the bar of the St. Louis airport about the time when Nanette Fabray came into the audience and sat on his lap, New Year's Eve, The Mark Hopkins Hotel, San Francisco

On Sunday he stuffed the frig with dungeness crabs

You can find the quilts of St. Louis women patched with real chipmunks and birds in the Jefferson museum next to the Lindbergh collection "Nothing like flying across the Atlantic in a one-seater" he said, "When she rocks, you rock, when you thrust so does she, and when she dives it's as if your soul bought the circus and you owned all the ferris wheels, *The Spirit of St. Louis!*"

A black man wrote a song about a St. Louis woman that go Hello Central, give me five o'nine, hello central give me five o' nine, the St. Louis woman said she liked my line about a man entering a woman's love pond, she thought i said love mine.

like a Mississippi school boy loves his mint and rye i love to see that evening sun go down when the St. Louis women come calling around

Many St. Louis women are from Kansas City

> The year was 1914
> W. C. Handy wrote a ragtime march with a blues
> tango introduction (The Tango, derived from
> the African Tangenda, was once banned all the
> way down to the Argentinian South Pole)
> but there was something missing.
> "What this music needs is a Vamp," the trombonist
> said, and that's how "St. Louis Woman" came into
> being
> The big publishers wouldn't chance her
> They were only interested in Whiteman's blues
> and so, at the age of 40, W. C. Handy went to
> bat for his Vamp, publishing 10,000
> copies of "St. Louis Blues" at his own expense

Handy flew up the Fatty Grimes diamond
from Memphis and presented it to her
(Hippolite's "Mystical Marriage")
He chauffeured her across the nation in
a whale-length white cadillac like the
one i once saw Bob Hope get out of
He introduced her to a Carnegie Hall
sell-out audience which she delighted
with her shanty-town ways
Sometimes she was as icy as the Portage glacier
in Portage, Alaska,
at other times she was tropical as the
Miami airport at 5:30 when the Santeria
jets sweep in

Resting under that mellow creole
river in a silver satin slip
the color of an enshrined coronet
mooning on the silky meat of a giant
clam
guarded by chocolate dandies
Irises on their creamy waistcoats
and a Tennessee billygoat covered with
cowrie shells
St. Louis Woman

Bitter Chocolate

I
Only the red-skins know what
I know, and they ain't talkin
So I keep good friends with
turkey whiskey
Or try to do some walkin
Don't want no lovin
Ain't anxious to play
And you want to know how
I got that way
Bitter Chocolate
Bitter Chocolate
Blood like ice water
Kisses taste like snuff
Why are all of my women
so jive and full of stuff

They call me a runaway father
But they won't give me no job
They say I'm a thief
when I'm the one gettin
robbed
Most of me was missing when
They brought me back from
Nam
My mama and my sister
cried for me
But my government didn't give
a damn
Bitter Chocolate
Bitter Chocolate
Sullied and sullen black
man

II

When they come to lynch somebody
Always breaking down my door
When they lay somebody off
I'm the first one off the floor
Bitter Chocolate
Bitter Chocolate
Veins full of brine
Skin sweatin turpentine
Cold and unfriendly
Got ways like a lizard

III

Well, it's winter in Chicago on
a February day
O'Hare airport is empty and
I call you on the line
It's 9:00 a.m. where you are
and the phone rings seven times
Hello, who is this? you say
in a sleeping heaving sigh
Your woman in the background yells
Who in the hell is that guy
Bitter Chocolate
Bitter Chocolate
I'm standing in the rain
All my love is all squeezed
out
All that I can give is pain
All that I can give is pain

The Smiley School

July 2, 1982—Juneau. Today the Rotterdam is in port. "We don't make any money from tourists," Andy says. "They just come into town, buy trinkets, and return to their ship." Randall Ackley is driving me to the Lemon Creek jail, where I instruct my class of two: Cornboy and Sanchez. Cornboy writes about the town in Iowa, where people drive tractors on the highway and wear levi shorts. "The midwestern maize grows as tall as a basketball player," Cornboy says. Cornboy says he knows more about the Eagle Dance than the Indians.

Sanchez writes about Nam. His lines crackle and ignite as though they were participants in a literary firefight. They bite like the pesky snake the Ghanians called "Dead Yesterday," it was so quick. His invective is as violent as the black G.I. he told us about, who splattered the mess hall walls with officers' brains. "I dunno, he just went berserk. Docile one minute, like a park deer, next minute, a mad minute."

In the lower forty-eight, the jails are filled with blacks.

Mexican Americans, Puerto Ricans, Cubans and Indians. Up here in Lemon Creek it's Eskimos and Indians.

Randall's Swedish grandmother lives in Sweden. For her, the Italians, French, and British are black people. The Irish, descendants of a crew whose fishing boat wandered too far from the coast of North Africa. Like the Smiley family. The Smileys were part Indian and part black. They didn't want to go to the black school, and they didn't want to go to the Indian school and so down in North Carolina there's a white school, a black school, and a Smiley school.

July 1st 1982

What do you do in a town where
11:00 p.m. looks like noon
and the streets are deserted
What do you do in a town
where space is so tight that
people build houses on boggy ground
or beneath avalanche-prone mountains
covered with Holstein hides
Suicide the therapist said at
Auke Lake
There's suicide up here
knifings in bars
Alcoholism
Up here it's like the
war without the sound effects
In the Viet Nam War
58,000 Americans died by homicide
59,000 Americans died by suicide

Ice Age

Like a gargantuan tongue, coated blue from the millions of tons of pressure, a man decapitating ice monster, calving upon those who defy it the Mendenhall Glacier glowers at visitors from where it lies, pouring forth into a sapphire colored pool, at Tongass National Forest. Two tipsy soldiers, intoxicated from Ranier Ale (green death) wandered too close to it and were "eaten." Like all of Yeil's creatures, it contracts in anger from the teenaged jeers, and beer cans, lying upon its great white royal coat, extending backwards to hundreds of miles

The glacialist warned them. The young glacialist said that all of Yeil's creatures demand respect, but the City Elders laughed at the glacier's impudence and the glacialist's hippie clothes

On the last day of Juneau the sky was as blue as a Harlem Monday. Small planes squatted upon the water like mosquitoes, Alaska's state bird

A ship, the Royal Viking, reposed majestically in the port as its baby boats ferried people into the city

At Dingby Dave's the folks were enjoying the clam chowder that was hot from start to finish

Exiled New Englanders were trying out their new indoor tennis courts, and transplanted Californians were in the sauna.

People were chatting and tasting smoked salmon behind Robert's Mountain

The guys and gals were hoisting a few in the Red Dog Saloon

Cars were lined up for a half-mile as passengers awaited their turn at

mining for McNuggets at the new McDonald's

In the House of Wickersham tourists were sampling the flaming sourdough and a mother spanked her son for tinkering with the Chickering grand piano, the one that Judge Wickersham brought from Baranof castle in Sitka. Inside the Lemon Creek jail, the prisoners

were having a potlatch supper of muk tuk seal fat seal oil herring eggs
smoked salmon and halibut cheeks

The congregation of the Russian Orthodox Church was split
down the middle

Some wanted to remain loyal to Moscow, others wanted inde-
pendence (the Catholic Bishop for the area dresses like a lumberjack)

All at once, the sky grew as white as Alaska Cotton
as the Mendenhall Glacier fired its frozen chunks upon
the town
The only exit from Juneau is by air
but nobody would be flying that day
The Bears prayed to the Bear God
the mountain goats climbed higher
and from his shack in the mountains
the glacialist's eyes followed the
Mendenhall glacier as it
crept towards Canada

But Nobody Was There

I heard a crying child in the other room
I entered the room, but nobody was there
I heard a spider crawl across the silverware
I opened the drawer, but nobody was there
I heard your steps creeping up the stairs
I opened the door, but nobody was there
But nobody was there, but nobody, but nobody
But nobody was there

I saw your spirit sitting in a chair
I turned my head, but nobody was there
I heard a knock and the doorknob turned
I answered the door, but nobody was there
I saw my love in her funeral bier
I turned on the lights, but nobody was there
But nobody was there, but nobody, but nobody
But nobody was there

I heard your laughter on the summer's air
I called your name, but nobody was there
I saw you bare, riding your favorite black mare
I ran to the woods, but nobody was there
I saw you by the moon, you were combing your
hair, I rushed outside, but nobody was there
But nobody was there, but nobody, but nobody
But nobody was there

Slaveship, German Model

I

A pout is a thing with scales
Even when gliding across a marble
floor and tailored by Adolfo
I am in a room of pouts
the clothes they wear would set me
back three months rent
     Off camera, he displays a mink ring
     On camera, he talks about his
     "disenfranchisement
     his oppression"; a word that once
had its hand out has gone and gotten
a manicurist

II

He said that he bought a Mercedes
because the holes on the side
reminded him of a slaveship

At the entrance to J.F.K.
there should be a sign:
"Welcome to New York
a rhetoric delicatessen"

Lake Bud

Lake Merritt is Bud Powell's piano
The sun tingles its waters
Snuff-jawed pelicans descend
tumbling over each other like
Bud's hands playing Tea For Two
or Two For Tea

Big Mac Containers, tortilla chip, Baby Ruth
wrappers, bloated dead cats, milkshake
cups, and automobile tires
float on its surface
Seeing Lake Merritt this way is
like being unable to hear
Bud Powell at Birdland
Because people are talking
Clinking glasses of whiskey and
shouting
"Hey, waiter"

Home Sweet Earth

Home Sweet Earth
Home Sweet Earth
Our first class berth in space
Stomping ground of the human race
Designer of Dorothy Dandridge's face
Of siamese cats, and Max Roach sets
Of beaches, incredibly sandy
Home Sweet Earth
Home Sweet Earth
Your waters are chicken soup
To our souls
You give us goldenrod and
Breakfast rolls
Italian spaghetti and Dizzy
Gillespie
Zimbabwe, and Lady Day
Home Sweet Earth
Home Sweet Earth
Thank you for French Fries
and Creme de Menthe
For Rock and Roll
For the Super Bowl
For scallops and the Alps
For George Clinton's funk
For Thelonius Monk
For Trumpets and trombones
For the Cathedral of Cologne
For Ka.Bah's black stone
Home Sweet Earth
Home Sweet Earth
Mother of legba and Damballah
Of kinky haired Jesus

Of Muhammed and Gautama
Of Confucius, and Krishna
Of Siva and Vishnu
Home Sweet Earth
Home Sweet Earth
May you be shamrock green again
May you stay out of the way of
Black holes
May you spin forever without
End
May you survive the nuclear deals
May you survive the chemical spills
May you survive the bio-technology
May you survive the peckerwood theology
May the Big Crunch theory be all wet!
May you survive man
May you survive man
Home Sweet Earth
Home Sweet Earth
You give us something to stand on

I'm Running For The Office Of Love

I'm running for the office of love
My heart is in the ring
I'm bad at making speeches
So I guess I'll have to sing
A tune of moons and flowers
And things that go with Spring
And things that go with Spring

Love is so political
I don't remember it this way
They'll curse you if you play it straight
And kill you if you're gay
They say that love is dangerous
That it's best to do without
So somebody has to speak for love
That's why I'm singing out

I'm running for the office of love
My heart is in the ring
I'm bad at making speeches
So I guess I'll have to sing
A tune of moons and flowers
And things that go with Spring
And things that go with Spring

Love is like a loaded gun
A fool stands in its way
There was one man who was on the run
He was trying to get away
But love took careful aim at him
She brought him in her sights
He bought her wine and perfume

And all her favorite delights
He hadn't been paying attention
And given love her due
She took away his peace of mind
And plagued him with the blues
I'm running for the office of love
My heart is in the ring
I'm bad at making speeches
So I guess I'll have to sing
A tune of moons and flowers
And things that go with Spring
And things that go with Spring

They say that love is dangerous
It's on the radio
That holding hands is fatal
A kiss can bring you low
The papers they keep shouting
That "LOVE MEANS DOOM AND GLOOM"
So love is lying low for awhile
Until her next big bloom
Until her next big bloom

I'm running for the office of love
My heart is in the ring
I'm bad at making speeches
So I guess I'll have to sing
A tune of moons and flowers
And things that go with Spring
And things that go with Spring

Life Is A Screwball Comedy

Life is a screwball comedy
life is a screwball comedy
It's Cary Grant leaning too
far back in a chair
It's Bill Cosby with a
nose full of hair
It's Richard Pryor
with his heart on fire
Life is a screwball comedy
life is a screwball comedy
It's Moms Mabley leaving her
dentures home
It's the adventures of Hope and Bing
It's Bert Williams doin' a buck and wing
It's Stepin Fechit sauntering before
a mule
It's matches in your shoes
It's April Fool
Life is a screwball comedy
Life is a screwball comedy
It's Scatman Crothers with his
sexy grin
It's W. C. Fields with a bottle
of gin
It's Maggie gettin' in her digs
at Jiggs
It's Desi and Lucy having a doozy
of a fight
It's Pigmeat Martin and Slappy White
Life is a Screwball Comedy
Life is a Screwball Comedy
It's Will Rogers twirling a rope

It's Buster Keaton wearing his
famous mope
It's Fatty Arbuckle in a leaking
boat
It's a scared rabbit
And a tricky Coyote
Life is a screwball comedy
Life is a screwball comedy
It's Eddie Murphy's howl
It's Whoopie Goldberg's stroll
It's Fred Allen's jowls
Its Pee-Wee Herman's clothes
It's Hardy giving Laurel a hard time
It's Chaplin up on his toes
Life is a screwball comedy
life is a screwball comedy
life is a screwball comedy
And the joke's on us

ISHMAEL REED grew up in working-class neighborhoods in Buffalo, New York. He attended Buffalo public schools and the University of Buffalo. As well as being a novelist, poet, and essayist, he is a song-writer, television producer, publisher, magazine editor, playwright, and founder of the Before Columbus Foundation and There City Cinema, both of which are located in Northern California. Among his honors, fellowships, and prizes is the Lewis H. Michaux Literary Prize awarded to him in 1978 by the Studio Museum in Harlem. He has taught at Harvard, Yale, and Dartmouth and for twenty years has been a lecturer at the University of California at Berkeley. He lives in Oakland, California.